AF578851

The Dance of the Divinity

Demystifying the Bhagwat Gita Vol-III

By Amit Kulshreshtha

Book Title: **The Dance of the Divinity**
Book Author: **Amit Kulshreshtha**
Series Name: **Demystifying the Bhagvad Gita, Volume-III**

Published by: **Amit Kulshreshtha**
Flat Number 1, Harmony Apartment, C58/16, Sector 62, Noida. Dist. Gautam Buddha Nagar, Uttar Pradesh -201301
Published in Noida, India

Printed and bound by: **Print-O-Tech**
C393, Sector 10, Noida,
Dist. Gautam Buddha Nagar, Uttar Pradesh -201301

This edition published: **August 2022**
ISBN **978-93-5680-667-2**

Copyright © 2022 Amit Kulshreshtha
This work is licensed under
Attribution-ShareAlike 4.0 International
https://creativecommons.org/licenses/by-sa/4.0/

You are free to:
Share — copy and redistribute the material in any medium or format
Adapt — remix, transform, and build upon the material for any purpose even commercially

Under the following terms:

Attribution — You must give appropriate credit, provide a link to the license, and indicate if changes were made. You may do so in any reasonable manner, but not in any way that suggests the licensor endorses you or your use.

ShareAlike — If you remix, transform, or build upon the material, you must distribute your contributions under the same license as the original.

उपद्रष्टानुमन्ता च भर्ता भोक्ता महेश्वरः |
परमात्मेति चाप्युक्तो देहेऽस्मिन्पुरुषः परः || Geeta 13.22 ||

Observer and permitter, supporter, enjoyer, great Lord and also the supreme Self : thus is said to be in this body the supreme Purusha. (13.22)

This work is dedicated to the infinite consciousness, the Absolute

Amit Kulshreshtha

Cover Picture Information

(Cover Picture:. Shri Krishna playing flute with gopis, ca. 1790—1800, Guler/Kangra region., Gouche and Gold on paper, Unknown artist;

Source: https://asia.si.edu/object/F1930.83/

Licensing information:

CC0 - CREATIVE COMMONS (CC0 1.0)
This image is in the public domain (free of copyright restrictions). You can copy, modify, and distribute this work without contacting the owner.

Table of Contents

Introduction 1

13. Matter and Spirit 5

Introduction 5

Key Terms 6

Chapter Summary 7

Analysis: 10

The Field and the Knower of the Field: 11

Field and its Distortions: 12

The True Knowledge: 13

The Object of True Knowledge 18

The Supreme as The Purusha 19

More about Prakriti and Purusha 23

Three Kinds of Bodies 24

More about Purusha and Prakriti 26

The four paths to self knowledge: 27

The World as an Interplay of Objects and the Subject: 27

An important inference from Verse 13.5 29

Original Sanskrit with Word Meanings, Transliteration and Translation (Chapter-13) 31

14. The Nature and its Three Gunas 49

Introduction 49

Chapter Summary 50

Analysis: 52

Introduction: 52

Supreme as the Father and Mother of All: 53

The Three Gunas Model of Prakriti: 54
The Three Gunas: 57
Mutual Action and Predominance of Gunas: 58
Effect of Gunas at the time of Death: 58
Summary of Effect of Guna: 59
Importance of going beyond Guna: 59
Going beyond the Gunas to get Immortality: 59
Summary of discussion: 62
Original Sanskrit with Word Meanings, Transliteration and Translation (Chapter-14) 66

5. The Supreme Primeval Man 77

Introduction: 77
Chapter Summary: 78
Analysis: 80
The Path to The Primaeval Purusha 81
The nature of Jiva (beings) 82
How Lord dwells in the body and departs it. 83
Manifestations of God: 84
The light of all lights 84
He Sustains all Life: 85
The Digestive Fire in all Animals: 85
Lord is the Self of all Creatures: 86
Supreme beyond perishable and the imperishable 86
Original Sanskrit with Word Meanings, Transliteration and Translation (Chapter-15) 92

16. The Divine and the Demonic Mind 101
Introduction: 101
Chapter Summary: 102
Analysis: 104
People have Divine and Demonic Qualities 104

Divine qualities lead to liberation: ... 105
Demonic qualities lead to bondage ... 106
Consequences of Demonic qualities ... 106
The Carnal world view: ... 107
Demonic people are enemies of the self and the world ... 108
The intention is more important than the act itself: ... 108
The Three Gates of the Hell: ... 108
Original Sanskrit with Word Meanings, Transliteration and Translation (Chapter-16) ... 110

17. Three Kinds of Faith ... 121
Introduction ... 121
Chapter Summary: ... 122
Key Terms: ... 124
Analysis: ... 126
Those Full of Faith are Guided by their Nature: ... 126
Worship by the three categories of people: ... 128
Three kinds of people and their choices regarding food, worship, austerity and charity : ... 128
Food: ... 128
Worship (Deeds): ... 128
Austerities of Body, Speech, and Mind: ... 129
The three Kinds of Austerities According to Guna ... 131
Threefold Nature of the Donations: ... 131
Going Beyond the Three Qualities: ... 132
Original Sanskrit with Word Meanings, Transliteration and Translation (Chapter-17) ... 134

18. Liberation through Renunciation ... 147
Introduction: ... 147
Key words: ... 147
Chapter Summary: ... 148

Attaining Absolute Freedom from Action and State of Brahm: 152

The Advice of Lord Krishna to Arjuna: 153

Analysis:: 154

The True Sanyasa: 154

Original Sanskrit with Word Meanings, Transliteration and Translation (Chapter-18) 173

Epilogue 203

Annexure-I 211

Pronunciation Guide for Verses 211

Vowels 211

Consonants: 212

Irregular Consonant Clusters 215

Introduction

The first step in gaining supreme knowledge about God is to understand oneself. First six chapters of the Bhagavad Gita deal with the objective of understanding the true nature of the self. "Demystifying the Bhagavad Gita (Vol-I): Understanding the self" is based on the first six chapters of the Bhagavad Gita to help readers understand this ancient wisdom with modern knowledge. The second volume titled "Glimpses of the Absolute" covers the next six chapters, from chapter 7 to chapter 12 of the Bhagavad Gita.

This book is a sequel to "Demystifying the Bhagavad Gita (Vol-II): Glimpses of the Absolute". In the second Volume, we learn that God has two-fold nature of the God, where his upper nature is pure consciousness and is beyond space and time, while the lower nature comprises of the five element world consisting of solid, liquid, gas, space, and heat. This becomes a little incomprehensible and therefore to meditate upon God one needs a symbolic representation. We then learnt about the sublime mystery of the Absolute revealed by Lord himself, explaining how the entire material world is created, pervaded, maintained and annihilated by the consciousness, the upper nature of God. Then we learnt how to contemplate divine presence in the countless objects in the universe and in mythological symbols. Then we learnt that in Vishwaroop or Universal form, everything in the universe is seen as contained in the Supreme. Beholding the Supreme in every form of the universe and the universe in the Supreme is seeing the Universal form.

In the last chapter of volume -2, we learnt the two paths to achieve the Supreme. In the first, one contemplates upon the Supreme who is formless and eternal, and in the second, one contemplates upon the Lord having form, and considering oneself a part of Him. The second approach is defined as bhakti yoga.

Proceeding ahead from the last chapter of volume 2, where God is seen in every space-time element, and considering oneself as part of that, the nature of the space-time world is discussed in detail. The space-time world manifested or unmanifested has been termed as Prakriti, which can be loosely translated as nature. The manifested nature, which was created in the past is perceivable because of the consciousness in the beings. The unmanifested may manifest in future or may remain unmanifested for the animals or humans forever. The present space-time world is visible to us because of the interaction of our sensory inputs received from nature with consciousness. True nature of the God can be considred as comprising of Purush (consciousness) and Prakriti as described in chapter 7 of volume -2 as upper and lower nature or it can be perceived as a field and the knower of the field as described in chapter 13 of this volume.

Lord then proceeds to explain the ***Prakriti*** in detail in chapter 14, where the three constituents of the manifested nature – Satwik Guna, Rajasik Guna, and Tamasik Guna are described.

In chapter 15, Purusha, the upper nature of the God is discussed in detail, wher we understand that how He as our awareness creates, sustains and destroy the beings and is root of everything manifested and unmanifested.

Chapter 16 discussed about how the divine and the demonic mind can liberate or bind a person and make her life worth living or miserable.

Chapter 17 elaborates Shraddha or faith is one of an essential element for liberating one from the bondage of the Karma, but faith alone, without the mystical knowledge of the scriptures, cannot liberate one from the fruit of his action. Unless one understands that the invisible, formless, eternal Supreme is the only truth, and is aware of this (***AUM TAT SAT)*** while doing every action including sacrifice, austerity and charity, the actions bind one to the fruit of such acts and the subject cannot liberate.

In chapter 18, Lord elaborates the importance of ***tyaga*** and ***sanyasa.*** The closest English translation of these words is renunciation and relinquishment, respectively. this being the last discourse, Lord sums up the whole doctrine of the Gita. It also sums up the entire Vedantic philosophy. Explaining the difference between renunciation and relinquishment, Lord says that renouncing is giving up the activities driven by desires, while relinquishing means surrendering the fruits of actions. Although one cannot abandon activities as they are part of the process of living, one must give up the results of her actions, asserts Lord Krishna. Lord also links the philosophy of Tri-Guna (three attributes theory) to the deeds of an individual and explains how these acts, under the influence of three attributes, bind one to the results if one does not transcend beyond three qualities (Triguna). Lord emphasises not on renouncing actions but giving up deeds with desire

Ms. Ayushi and Deepali Kulshreshtha deserve a thankful mention for their contribution in designing the cover of the book. Author is also pleased to acknowledge the efforts of Ms. Deepali Kulshreshtha for proofreading, and finalizing the content and titke of the book.

13. Matter and Spirit

God is spirit, and his worshipers must worship in the Spirit and in truth.

-John 4.24

Introduction

The purpose of this chapter is to understand the body and the Spirit and their differences. Additionally, it discusses the subject matter of the knowledge, and also about whom it is.

Chapter seven examined two attributes of the Supreme- the upper, and the lower nature. The lower nature, forming the three qualities (Gunas), divided into eightfold elements, makes the universe, while the upper one is the life force itself.

In the present chapter, we find two new terms- field and its knower. Metaphorically, the field is the physical universe or the body of a being, while the Self is its knower.

Discriminating between the two, Lord describes wisdom about the Self and the Prakriti according to Samkhya. Samkhya philosophy defines the knower of the field as Purusha (the Self) and the Field as Prakriti (Matter).

The first verse of the chapter, the question of Arjuna about the difference between Prakriti and Purush, field and its knower, knowledge and the objects of it is not present in all the versions and is numbered as zero here.

Key Terms

Some key terms must be understood to have a true insight into the chapter. These terms may not have the same meaning as they have today, we should keep in mind that the words in any language evolve gradually and may mean different over a different period. The same word may have a different meaning at different places, as is very common in poetry.

kShetra: The word Kshetra(क्षेत्र; Itrans: **kShetra**) means the field in Sanskrit. Here in this chapter, it has been used for the bodies of the beings to explain the principles of Samkhya Yoga.

kshetragya: (क्षेत्रज्ञ, Itrans: kSetraj~na): It is the pervasive, genderless, infinite, conscious, eternal truth, and bliss, and which does not change, yet is the cause of all changes and creation. It is synonymous to Barham, or the Supreme. Simply put, it is the God of the Bible and Allah of the Quran.

mahAbhUta: (महाभूत, Itrans: mahAbhUta): The five basic elements constituting the physical visible world. They are solids symbolised as earth, liquids as water, gases as air, emptiness as space, and heat as fire respectively.

avyakta: (अव्यक्त:(Avyakt is the unmanifested material cause of the universe. Everything in nature is not observed by our senses, maybe because of its size, wavelength, frequency or any other nature. Some objects are perceived by us differently from what they are. For example, light is a kind of electromagnetic wave but appears to us as colourful in the range of the visible spectrum. Electromagnetic waves beyond the visible spectrum are unmanifested therefore and are manifested differently in their visible spectrum range.

Atoms constituting the matter are mostly emptiness, still, they look and feel like solid. The matter appears different from what it is. The void in these cases is unmanifested or avyakt.

Chapter Summary

While reading the chapter, we encounter two new terms: kshetra and khsetragya. Kshetra is the physical body of a being. Kshetragya, the Knower of the Field, on the other hand, is the one who knows about the body. Introducing at the beginning of the chapter, Lord Krishna states that this body is the Field, and the one who knows the Field from head to toe is the Knower of the Field. He, himself is the Knower of the Field in all the Fields, Lord declares further. Wisdom about the Field and the Knower of the Field is the real wisdom.

These terms appear very similar to Prakriti and Purush, the terms used in Samkhya philosophy and also discussed in chapter two, where Prakriti is the matter, and the Purush is the Universal Spirit. Purusha is an entity beyond space-time dimension and responsible for all life, the cause of experiences, emotions, consciousness and intelligence in all beings.

Describing the Field (body) Lord says that it consists of five great elements, namely solid, liquid, gas, heat, and space. These five elements of the physical world together with intellect and ego and the un-manifested and the eleven senses. The breakup of eleven senses is as follows: Five for acquiring information: the eyes, ears, nose, tongue and skin, the five working senses: voice, legs, hands, anus and genitals and the mind, which is within and which can be called the sense within. Therefore, including the mind, there are eleven senses altogether. Then there are five objects of the senses; smell, taste, sight, touch and sound. The aggregate of these twenty-four elements is called the field of activity. Further, there are emotions such as desire, hatred, happiness and distress, which are interactions of the five great elements in the gross body.

Humility, modesty, nonviolence, forbearance, simplicity, listening to the teacher, cleanliness, steadiness and self-control are the attributes of a wise person. More qualities of such a person include a renunciation of the objects of sense gratification, absence of false ego, constant reflection on the agony inherent in birth like death, old age and disease. Additionally, such a person is not attached to children, wife, and home; has equanimity amid pleasant and unpleasant events; has unwavering and unalloyed devotion to the supreme; loves solitude, and has a distaste for social groups. Some additional marks of a wise person are Constancy in the Wisdom of the Self, understanding of the object of essential wisdom. What is contrary to these are the signs of an ignorant person.

Thus describing the Feld, Knower of the Field and the Knowledge, Lord Krishna explains the object of the knowledge, i.e. the Supreme himself. He says that the Supreme is beginningless and is neither real (sat) nor unreal (asat). He has hands and feet everywhere; eyes, head and face all over, listening all, he dwells in the world in every particle. He is the perceiver of all senses, unattached yet the sustainer of all, devoid of all Gunas (qualities), yet enjoying all Gunas(qualities). He is inside as well as outside of all beings, living and non-living. He is subtle, near as well as far away and is undivided yet appears divided in beings. He is the object of knowledge and is creator, sustainer and destroyer of all beings. He, the light of all lights, is said to be beyond the darkness. He is the wisdom, the object of knowledge, seated in the hearts of all, and reached through wisdom itself. Knowing this, one attains the abode of the Supreme.

Further, the Lord talks about Prakriti(Nature) and the Purusha(Spirit, or Consciousness). Lord says Nature and the Consciousness both are beginningless and that all manifestations and qualities arise from nature. He says the nature is instrumental in creation, cause and effect and the Consciousness or Spirit is instrumental in experiencing pleasure and pain. Consciousness associating with Nature enjoys the Gunas(qualities) born out of nature. Attachment of a being to these Gunas(qualities) is the cause of birth in different species.

Observer and permitter, supporter, enjoyer, great Lord and also the supreme Self: thus is said to be in this body the Consciousness. Knowing the Nature with its three qualities, and the SELF, one gets rid of the sufferings of birth and death.

Some by meditation, see the Self in the Self by the Self, while the others by the Samkhya Yoga, and some others by the Yoga of Action.

Yet, some others, ignorant of the true nature of the Self, having heard of it from others, begin to worship;

and these also transcend death, believing to what they have heard.

Lord says further that all living beings are born due to the union of Prakriti (matter) and the Purusha (Spirit) and the same supreme Lord as the Consciousness resides equally within all perishable beings. The one who knows this knows the truth.

Therefore, those seeing indeed everywhere the same Lord equally dwelling in all beings, even when killing opponents in the just war, they do not destroy the SELF by the SELF, and thus tread the highest Path. Understanding this, they perceive that Gunas(qualities) are performing all actions, and they are not the doer.

When one perceives all being having the same Spirit, one reaches the place of the Eternal Supreme. Eternal Supreme is beginningless and not non-destructible. Though sitting in every being, He is the cause of every action, but as a consequence of actions, He is not affected. One can understand this by the example that as the all-pervading space is not tainted because of its subtlety, similarly the Self, seated in everybody, remains untainted. As the one sun illuminates the whole world, so the Supreme Self, the knower of the field illuminates all Fields (all beings), They who by the eye of Wisdom perceive this difference between the Field and the Knower of the Field, and the liberation of beings from Matter(Nature), they go to the Supreme.

Analysis:

The Field and the Knower of the Field:

The Lord says this body is a Field and the one who knows this is the Knower of the Field. Why Lord describes the bodies of living beings as a field? Similar to a Field, fruits of actions are reaped in it. Probably also because it was a commonly known thing fit for an analogy to elucidate a complex subject. If the body is analogous to a Field, then the one who fully comprehends the body perceives it as different from himself, is the Knower of the Field.

Lord further unambiguously declares that He, himself is the Knower of the Field in all Fields. You may note that when Lord says " I am the knower of the field in all fields", he means by himself as not a worldly being, not an entity of space-time dimension, but the Spirit that is the real subject of all the senses and feelings, the one who is responsible for emotions. That Supreme Self is the Knower of the Field in all Fields.

The body is the Field in which events such as birth, growth, decline and death take place. The Consciousness, the Spirit, the Self remains inactive and detached, which lies behind all active states as a witness. The witness is not the individual mind but the eternal consciousness which does not require mind and senses for witnessing. He is the awareness, the Knower of all objects.

Lord further declares that He is going to teach about the Field, its distortions, and also about its Knower. Several philosophers (Rishis) have described it with numerous hymns full of reasoning.

Field and its Distortions:

Five great elements constituting the universe are solids symbolised as earth, liquids as water, gases as air, emptiness as space, and heat as fire respectively. Anything in the cosmos is either one or a combination of these ingredients. However, for us, our world is not only the mundane physical universe formed of these five great elements, but also a vibrant world consisting of our egos, thoughts, feelings, enchanting landscapes, tasty and aromatic food, and warm touch of our loved ones. A product of our mind, this world is our mental construct. The elements of its construction are nineteen subtle elements, classified in four groups, a group of four mental organs mind, intellect, egoism, and the unmanifest, five senses of knowledge, five senses of action, and five pastures of sense organs.

The literature classifies mind as the eleventh sense organ classified under both, the senses of action and the senses of knowledge. Intellect is the power of reasoning, egoism is the false sense of self, and the unmanifest is the power of Supreme, which causes, wisdom, egoism and power of the mind.

Five sense organs of knowledge give information to mind. They are eyes, ears, nose, tongue, and skin. They provide information about the physical world.

Five sense organs for actions are voice, hands, legs, the anus and the genitals. In this way, there are ten sense organs. We also have eleventh sense organ as mind (manas) which is both, knowledge sense organ and action sense organ responsible for thoughts and determination. Verse 13.5 thus describes a total of eleven sense organs.

Additionally, there are five pastures of sense as the scene, sound, taste, smell and feel. All these combined are nineteen subtle and five great elements (i.e. twenty-four) described in Samkhya philosophy, constituting the Field (body or universe).

Giving rise to desire, aversion, pleasure, pain, intelligence and courage, the interaction among these elements distorts the body and is expressed as the Field and its distortions.

The True Knowledge:

After discussing the distortion of the physical body as a result of the interaction of twenty-four elements, Lord Krishna describes the virtues that are acquired as a result of Self-knowledge or are conducive to attain it. These virtues are essential to obtain real knowledge and to approach the Absolute Truth. They are not the result of the interaction of the elements, but a means of getting rid of the myriad magical web of them.

Let us understand how these virtues constitute real knowledge. The ability to identify oneself as different from the body, and to understand oneself as the true self is the fundamental knowledge. This knowledge gives rise to the virtues described here.

Humility is lack of pride. It means that one is not eager to be honoured by others. Concept of life rooted in materialism makes one keen to receive honour from others, but for a person in perfect knowledge -- who understands that she is not this body, honour or dishonour, of the body is meaningless.

Nonviolence generally means not killing or physically harming somebody. However, Lord also preaches Arjuna to fight the just war which may slay the humongous amount of people. Preaching nonviolence as essential virtue may appear contradictory, therefore, but is a tricky concept. While executing somebody as a duty to uphold the justice, the knowledgeable person does so as a duty, knowing fully well that she is merely destroying the body of the opponent as a duty, but not the real self. Lord has clarified it in 13.28

समं पश्यन्हि सर्वत्र समवस्थितमीश्वरम् ।

न हिनस्त्यात्मनात्मानं ततो याति परां गतिम् ||१३ - २९||

Seeing indeed everywhere the same Lord equally dwelling, he does not destroy the SELF by the self, and thus treads the highest Path.

When one mistakenly identifies oneself with the body, the materialistic needs resulting from the interaction of elements described in the previous section may take over their mind to prompt for the violence. In such cases, violent actions are not justified as the acts of the self to merely destroy the body.

On the other hand, a soldier, exterminating the opponent, while defending their motherland, is doing so as their rightful duty, destroying the body of the opponent, but not the real self.

Humility, modesty, nonviolence, forbearance, simplicity, listening to the teacher, cleanliness, steadiness and self-control are the attributes of a wise person. More qualities of such a person include a renunciation of the objects of sense gratification, absence of false ego, constant reflection on the agony inherent in birth like death, old age and disease. Additionally, such a person is not attached to children, wife, and home; has equanimity amid pleasant and unpleasant events; has unwavering and unalloyed devotion to the supreme; loves solitude, and has a distaste for social groups. Some additional marks of a wise person are Constancy in the Wisdom of the Self, understanding of the object of essential wisdom. What is contrary to these are the signs of an ignorant person.

Forbearance is patience and courage to bear the insult, dishonour or torture, which the knowledgeable persons understand, can affect their body and not their real existence.

Self-control is also the quality which promotes perfect knowledge and is also evident in the persons who achieve real wisdom. The drivers for lack of self-control are always the materialistic temptations driven by the delusional identification of oneself with the body. Learning perfect knowledge also requires self-control as the mind frequently diverts towards the pastures of the sense organs.

A teacher having perfect knowledge is often the best source of it. Sitting near him to learn is undoubtedly a means to acquire real knowledge.

Cleanliness means the absence of dirt, dust, stains, stinking smell. The goals of cleanliness are health, aesthetics etc. With the help of cleanliness, we keep our physical and mental health better, which makes us feel good. Maintaining cleanliness is an essential part of healthy living and helps us to improve our personality by keeping us externally and internally clean. It also brings positive thoughts in mind reducing or eliminating the occurrence of diseases. A healthy body is the abode of a healthy mind. No wonder, it is said that cleanliness is next to Godliness. The scriptures praise the virtue of cleanliness as a virtue needed to acquire perfect knowledge.

Indifference to the object of senses also emerges from the real understanding of the Self. One's sense organs, being part of the body, are different from one's actual existence as the Self. Charms of the physical world do not delude a person who can discriminate between physical and real existence and can understand that weakness, pain, diseases, old age, and death are the consequence of taking birth in this world. Practising indifference to the object of senses leads to the discriminating knowledge of the Self and the body.

Non-attachment is the absence of liking of the things. Affection is an intense form of attachment where one identifies with the other, such that the happiness or sorrow of one depends upon the other. Affinity with wife, son or home, money or designation is an indicator that one identifies oneself as body as these relations are regarding the body.

Attachments lead to further delusion and obstruct obtaining perfect knowledge where one identifies with the consciousness. Non-attachment leads to real wisdom, following which it is easier to achieve discriminatory wisdom between the body and the Self, which is the real knowledge. In the state of equanimity, one is not delighted in accomplishing the desirable and is also not disappointed on attaining the undesirable, which is also conducive to knowledge.

Unwavering meditation on the thought that only the Supreme in the form of Self exists, and whatsoever is perceived or not perceived is the Supreme, understanding oneself as the part of Him also leads to knowledge. Thinking this in solitude with a distaste for the company of people are the other methods to achieve true knowledge. Solitude helps in constant focus on these thoughts and is conducive to knowledge.

In summary, the false sense of the Self, giving rise to the ego, creates several distortions, such as desire, aversion, pleasure, pain, intelligence, and courage. These distortions create a veil between real Self and physical existence. They are impediments in the way of understanding the true nature of the Self and distinction between the body and the Self. Virtues such as humility, forbearance, self-control, desire to learn this complex special knowledge from the teachers, non-attachment, cleanliness, and equanimity help in abolishing false sense of ego and therefore help in the true understanding of the discriminatory knowledge between Self and the body. Further, when one comprehends the discrimination between Self and the body, the ego generated through the false sense of self, where one identifies oneself with the body and mind, readily disappears, and the virtues enumerated above appear to flow effortlessly in the behaviour of such individuals. These virtues are, therefore, elements of essential knowledge.

Constancy in the knowledge of the Self and understanding the elements of essential knowledge is declared to be the knowledge; all against it is ignorance, proclaims Lord Krishna.

The Object of True Knowledge

After knowing what the knowledge is, the question arises, about whom it is? Who is the object of the enlightenment? Answering the query Lord says that which is to be known, and whose knowledge can give immortality is the beginningless Brahm, the Supreme. Describing further, he says that Supreme Absolute is neither existent nor non-existent.

Beyond dimensions of space and time, the Supreme is the consciousness and the life force of all creatures. Unlike the objects of the space-time dimensions, he is beyond the perception of senses. As the Supreme does not exist in the space-time world, it is non-existent for the living beings who consider only those things to exist which their sense organs can detect directly or through some instrumentation.

The Supreme is also not non-existent, implying that it is existent because he is the cause of everything that exists. He, as the inner Self, is the subject of every observation. The awareness makes us perceive the pressure waves emanating from the throat of a singer, received through ears and transmitted to the brain as a melodious song, and the electromagnetic radiations emanating from a candle received through eyes as a yellow light. What we perceive as reality is a process involving the inner Self. The physical universe out there is a mental construct inside your mind, vividly projected as a result of interaction with the consciousness. The so-called existent universe is therefore non-existent, and the Supreme Consciousness is indeed that exists, but beyond the space-time world.

Further, The Supreme, being the subject of all perceptions, is himself beyond all observations. For an analogy, an eye sees the whole world, but cannot see itself. The fact that it beholds indicates its existence.

Similarly, the Supreme does not exist as our physical world. Nevertheless, the fact that we can observe and have feelings are evidence of the existence of a subject that receives our emotions and observations.

When it is said that the Supreme is beyond the physical existence, one may suppose him to be non-existent (asat), to be a void or non-entity. To counter this supposition Lord proceeds to declare that the Supreme exists as the inner Self-consciousness.

The Supreme as The Purusha

The concept of the Supreme as the inner Self, witnessing all and therefore called knower, and the body as the field, is similar to the idea that of Samkhya, Purusha being the Consciousness and the tangible nature as the Prakriti or object of the conscious subject.

According to the Samkhya, the universe came into existence due to the union of Consciousness (Purusha) and material Nature (Prakriti). Purusha is a Sanskrit word meaning man. Describing the Purusha, Lord says that Having hands and feet everywhere; having eyes, head, and face everywhere; all-hearing, He dwells in the world, enveloping all.

If the Purusha is the inner Self, having no form, origin, and qualities, then why the Lord describes Him as having numerous heads, eyes, and face everywhere?

The concept has its origin in the tenth book of Rigveda. First two verses of the Sukta are as follows

सहस्रशीर्षा पुरुषः सहस्राक्षः सहस्रपात |

सभूमिं विश्वतो वत्वीत्यतिष्ठद दशाङगुलम ||RV:10.90.1||

पुरुष एवेदं सर्वं यद भूतं यच्च भव्यम |

उतामृतत्वस्येशानो यदन्नेनातिरोहति ||RV:10.90.2||

sahasrashIrShA puruShaH sahasrAkShaH sahasrapAta |

sabhUmiM vishvato vartvAtyatiShThada dashA~Ngulama ||RV:10.90.1||

puruSha evedaM sarvaM yada bhUtaM yachcha bhavyama |

utAmrtatvasyeshAno yadannenAtirohati ||RV:10.90.2||

The Purusha has Thousands of Heads, Thousands of Eyes and Thousands of Feet (Thousand signifies innumerable). Enveloping the cosmos from all sides (i.e. He pervades each part of the Creation), and extends beyond in the Ten Directions (RV10.90.1)

The Purusha Sukta states that He pervades the entire universe and extends beyond that in all ten directions.

Permeating everything, conscious and unconscious, and poetically depicted as a being with thousands heads, eyes and legs, He is the inner Self of all beings. It is so because all heads, legs, and eyes of those creatures are his own. Enjoying all stimuli from the sense organs as their inner Self, he is the real subject of all sensual indulgences of all beings. Manifesting in all, that existed in the past and the future, he is the essence of the world.

Further to clarify that the description of the Supreme as having thousands of heads, hands, legs and eyes is just a metaphoric narrative, Lord explains the Supreme as devoid of the qualities yet the enjoyer of them, He is the perceiver of all sense objects without the senses. With imperceptible subtlety, He is inside as well as outside all creatures. Being within as the Consciousness of the animals, He is very near to them, still being inaccessible to their senses, He is far away from them.

The inner Self of all beings appears divided amongst them. However, one may recall that Consciousness is beyond space-time domain and cannot be separate, therefore. Being apart is a space-time quality because to qualify to be isolated, two things need to exist in different space or time coordinates.

As the life force, Consciousness creates and destroys all creatures and also sustains them by guiding them as inner awareness in the universe. Describing the Supreme, Lord, therefore, proclaims that Undivided yet appearing divided in beings, He the object of knowledge is the creator sustainer and destroyer of all. He, the light of all lights, is said to be beyond the darkness. Sitting in the hearts of all, He is the Wisdom, the object of Wisdom, and is reached by Wisdom.

Let us understand, why is Consciousness called the light of all lights? Beholding the sun, the moon, lighting or any other lighted object involves the following process of interpretation:

The glowing object emits tiny packets of electromagnetic energy, each consisting of electrical and magnetic pulses.

They strike the human retina. If the frequency of pulsation is between 400 billion to 800 billion cycles per second, their energy is just right to fire a stimulus to send signals to the neighbouring neurons in the human eye.

Neurons send the electrical signals to the optical lobe in the back of our brain and wow! You experience a brilliantly shining sunrise in front of you.

In other words, witnessing the magical sunrise is a complex process involving an interplay of sensual inputs and Consciousness.

The Supreme, residing in our hearts as the true Self or the Consciousness, is responsible for all our experiences. Enabling us to behold even the external luminescence, the radiance of the inner Self is rightly described as the light of the lights.

The Kathopnishad 2-2.15 elucidates this as follows

न तत्र सूर्यो भाति न चन्द्रतारकम्

नेमा विद्युतो भान्ति कुतोऽयमग्निः ।

तमेव भान्तमनुभाति सर्वं

तस्य भासा सर्वमिदं विभाति ॥ - काठकोपनिषत् २-२-१५

na tatra sUryo bhAti na chandratArakam nemA vidyuto bhAnti kuto.ayamagniH |

tameva bhAntamanubhAti sarvaM tasya bhAsA sarvamidaM vibhAti ||

The sun does not shine there, nor the moon and the stars, nor these lightnings-much less this fire. As He shines, everything shines after Him. By His light all this is lighted.

More about Prakriti and Purusha

As described in chapter 7, there are two natures of the Supreme -- inferior nature, the Prakriti, and superior nature, the Self or the Consciousness. Lord explains that both the Prakriti (matter) and the Spirit (the Self) are beginningless as they belong to the eternal Supreme. The supremacy of the Supreme is due to His possession of the two, the matter and the spirit, causing the creation, destruction, and sustenance of the world. Further, all the distortions explained in the previous section and qualities (Guna) originate from the Prakriti. Then what are the different forms originating from Prakriti?

Nature is the cause of effect, instrument, and agent, while the Purusha is the cause of experiencing pleasure and pain. The Self experiences the qualities(Guna) born out of Prakriti (matter), however, the ego mistakenly believes them as its experiences and gets attached to them. This fondness of the ego to the tempting objects causes rebirth of the creatures in the good and the inferior wombs.

Now the question arises that if the Self is eternal and unborn, and the physical body is destroyed after death, how a being takes rebirth?

Let us understand the theory of rebirth from the concept of three kinds of bodies, namely-- Physical body, subtle body and causal body.

Three Kinds of Bodies

Physical Body:

It consists of five great elements: solid, liquid, gas, heat, and space. It is accessible to senses and is therefore visible to you as well as others. It has limited natural life and ceases to exist beyond a specific age set by nature.

Subtle Body:

Much beyond our physical existence, our individuality consists of our thoughts, feelings, ego, likes, and dislikes etc. This idea of ourselves is, in fact, our subtle body. This reflects our personality, phobias, and attitude. We have talked about twenty-four elements of the Prakriti. Five great elements earth, water, air, fire and space are the components of the physical body. Remaining nineteen elements are the components of the subtle body as described in previous sections. They are -- five senses of knowledge(eyes, ear, nose, tongue and skin), five senses of action(voice, hands, feet, anus, genitals), five pastures of senses and four internal organs (mind, intellect, memory, and ego). The five senses of knowledge and the five senses of action are not the physical organs but the subtle ones responsible for perception and act. For example, one may close her eyes but can still daydream or visualise the objects through subtle eyes. Similarly, a person with amputated legs can still walk with the help of artificial limbs. Famous scientist, Stephan Hawking after the loss of his speech, was able to communicate through a speech-generating device – initially through use of a handheld switch, and eventually by using a single cheek muscle. What we mean with the voice as the part of the subtle body is the subtle voice, which even Hawking could speak despite his physical disability. In short the subtle body is a mental construct of oneself. The subtle body consisting of the nineteen elements is the one according to which we behave and act.

Causal body:

It is the most subtle body of the creatures. Nescience (avidya) of the real identity of the Self produces it. Containing the expressions and impressions of the previous life, it is the cause of rebirth. The Causal Body serves as the source from which the Subtle and Gross Body arises, and into which eventually the two bodies dissolve back. After the death, the causal body enters into a fetus and serves as a seed from which the new body arises. The causal body is the medium to transfer the unfulfilled passions, likes and dislikes into the new body so that its unaccomplished yearnings can be fulfilled.

Ignorance about the true nature of the Self creates the causal body at the time of death. The ignorance creates egoism that further produces distortions like desires, aversions, passions etc. The causal body saves these distortions and experiences of life at the time of death. Later on, it enters into an embryo of a suitable womb, where it finds potential to fulfil the cravings and urges of the past life. If the subject has realised her true Self, then as there is no ego, consequently, there is a complete absence of desires and passions. There is no need for the creation of a causal body to record life experiences in such cases, and the subject attains the abode of the Supreme.

More about Purusha and Prakriti

Lord further says that the Absolute is the Supreme Self in this body and is also Spectator, Permitter, Supporter, and Enjoyer.

The Great Lord is **Spectator** being a witness in the beings, though Himself not acting. Not taking part in the activities of the body, the Supreme Self is distinct from the body, observing it and its acts closely. Expressing approbation or satisfaction over the acts, the Supreme is also the **Permitter**. Despite not engaged in actions, while the body and senses are active, He seems to be working in co-operation with them. Simply witnessing as a bystander, he never stands in the ways of those engaged in their activities. Further, the Supreme Self is the **Supporter** as He enables mind and intellect to take care of itself. Additionally, He creates the ego to induce the instinct for survival.

Furthermore, enjoying all activities and indulgences of the beings, the Supreme Self is their real **Enjoyer**, not the physical existence as believed by the creatures. Consequent to the roles he plays as elaborated, He is also the **great Lord** and the **Supreme Self.**

He who knows Purusha and Prakrit together with their qualities is not born again, declares Lord Krishna. It is tough to understand the differences between the real

Self and the ego. Accomplishments leads to pride, falsely thinking oneself as the doer, and taking credit of it. One forgets that the real doer is the Prakriti acting because of its qualities and the power of Supreme Self. This discriminatory knowledge between Prakriti and Purusha is the source of wisdom that can eradicate the ego, the source of desire, aversion, passion and other distortions. Thus the cause of formation of the causal body is eliminated, and the person is not born again.

The four paths to self knowledge:

Describing four paths of self-knowledge, Lord says that some perceive the Self by meditating on the Self, others by Samkhya Yoga and still others by Karma Yoga. By continuous contemplation, the yogis behold the Self, in themselves by their intelligence. Still others following the path of Samkhya, reflect on the thoughts that the Self is a mere witness to the acts of Prakriti driven by its qualities, refine their mind and achieve Self-knowledge. Yet another path of Self-knowledge is Karma yoga.

Detaching oneself from the fruit of action Karma yogis behold the Self through purity achieved by their selfless actions. Yet others, not knowing the above three paths, learning by listening and sitting near a scholar and adhering to what they have heard, also cross beyond death and achieve the Self-knowledge.

The World as an Interplay of Objects and the Subject:

Werner Heisenberg, among others, interpreted mathematically to mean that reality doesn't exist until observed. Famous scientist John Weeler speculated that reality is created by observers in the universe. In the famous double-slit experiment, Light from a coherent source, such as laser beam falls on a photographic film through two parallel slits. The wave nature of light causes the light waves passing through the two slits to interfere, producing bright and dark bands on the screen – a result that would not be expected if light consisted of classical particles. Interestingly further, the interference pattern disappears if the photon detectors are used to determine which photon passed through which slit. In another variation of the double-slit experiment, which was suggested by John Wheeler, called the delayed-choice experiment, the interference pattern vanishes even if the photon detectors are placed after they have struck the screen. These experiments suggest that the observer is an essential part of the observations and physical reality is not independent to the conscious observer.

Same is echoed in verse 13.26 when the Lord says "Whatever is born, the unmoving or the moving, know thou, O best of the Bharatas, that to be owing to the union of Prakriti and Purusha." The world is the interplay of Consciousness and nature. What we perceive as reality is the projection of nature through sense organs in our mind (called as Maya in Vedanta) and interpreted as space-time reality by Consciousness.

The wise person understands that the Prakriti is the real doer acting according to its qualities, and the Self is the observer. Realising that the diversified existence rests on the Eternal One and have evolved from that Supreme alone, she reaches the Eternity. The all-pervading nature of the Supreme is absorbed into the innermost mind. One may presume that if the Supreme is the Self of all creature than He might get tainted by the acts of the individuals.

To clarify this, Lord further says that having no qualities, having no beginning, the Supreme Self neither acts nor tainted by the acts of the beings. As the mire cannot soil the all-pervading space due to its subtlety, similarly the deeds of a being cannot stain the omnipresent Self in it. Lord further illustrates the concept through the example of the sun. He says, as the sun illuminates the whole world, The Supreme Self illumines all bodies, including material beings, avyakt (the unmanifested material cause of the universe), moving and unmoving objects, and the twenty-four elements explained in previous sections. The Lord uses the example of the sun very cleverly to emphasise two things. First, as the single sun illuminates the whole world, the Supreme illuminates the numerous bodies in the universe. And the Second, as the light from the sun enables us to see the objects, similarly, the inner light of the Self enables us to perceive the world.

An important inference from Verse 13.5

महाभूतान्यहंकारो बुद्धिरव्यक्तमेव च |
इन्द्रियाणि दशैकं च पञ्च चेन्द्रियगोचराः ||१३- ५| ||

mahAbhUtAnyaha.nkAro buddhiravyaktameva cha .

indriyANi dashaika.n cha pa~ncha chendriyagocharAH ..

13\-5..

The verse also indicate about the number system in vougue during the time of Mahabharata. Use of numbers like five (panch) and dashek (ten and one) strongly suggest evidence of decimal number system being prevalent during the age. This is because the next number after ten is being pronounced as ten and one (dashaika). There are other refrences of numbers in the text. You may recall verse 7.3 reproduced below:

मनुष्याणां सहस्रेषु कश्चिद्यतति सिद्धये |
यततामपि सिद्धानां कश्चिन्मां वेत्ति तत्त्वतः ||७- ३||

manuShyANA.n sahasreShu kashchidyatati siddhaye .
yatatAmapi siddhAnA.n kashchinmA.n vetti tattvataH.

Scarcely one out of thousand of persons strives for perfection. Scarcely any one of the striving, truly understands Me. (7.03)

Use of numbers of base 10 such as dash, shat, sahastra (10, 100, 1000) and then getting successive numbers by using numbers from one to ten indicate the use of decimal number system which was prevalent much before Aryabhata (born in 476 CE)

Original Sanskrit with Word Meanings, Transliteration and Translation (Chapter-13)

अथ त्रयोदशोऽध्यायः । क्षेत्रक्षेत्रज्ञविभागयोगः

atha trayodasho.adhyAyaH |

kShetrakShetraGYaavibhAgayogaH

Here begins the thirteenth chapter (kShetrakShetraGYavibhAgayogaH)

अर्जुन उवाच ।
प्रकृतिं पुरुषं चैव क्षेत्रं क्षेत्रज्ञमेव च ।
एतद्वेदितुमिच्छामि ज्ञानं ज्ञेयं च केशव ॥१३- ०॥

arjuna uvAcha .

prakR^itiM puruSha.n chaiva kShetra.n kShetraGYameva cha .

etadveditumichchhAmi GYAnaM GYeya.n cha keshava .. 13\-0..

arjuna uvaacha = Arjuna said; prakR^itiM = nature;purushhaM = the enjoyer; cha = also; eva = certainly; kshetraM = the field; kshetraGYaM = the knower of the field; eva = certainly; cha = also; etat.h = all this; vedituM = to understand; ichchhaami = I wish; GYaanaM = knowledge; GYeyaM = the object of knowledge; cha = also; keshava = O KRishhNa

Arjun asked:

Nature and the essence of the nature, also the Field and the Knower of the Field, Wisdom and that which ought to be known, these I fain would learn, O Keshava.

श्रीभगवानुवाच ।
इदं शरीरं कौन्तेय क्षेत्रमित्यभिधीयते ।
एतद्यो वेत्ति तं प्राहुः क्षेत्रज्ञ इति तद्विदः ॥१३- १॥

shrIbhagavAnuvAcha .

idaM sharIraM kaunteya kShetramityabhidhIyate .

etadyo vetti taM prAhuH kShetraGYa iti tadvidaH .. 13\-1 ..

shriibhagavaan = Pronoun for Lord Krisha; uvaacha = said; idaM = this; shariiraM = body; kaunteya = O son of Kunti; kshetraM = the field; iti = thus; abhidhiiyate = is called; etat.h = this; yaH = one who; vetti = knows; taM = he; praahuH = is called; kshetraGYaH = the knower of the field; iti = thus; tatvidaH = by those who know this.

Lord Krishna said: O Arjuna, this body is called the field; and that which knows is called the knower of the field by the sages (13.01)

क्षेत्रज्ञं चापि मां विद्धि सर्वक्षेत्रेषु भारत |
क्षेत्रक्षेत्रज्ञयोर्ज्ञानं यत्तज्ज्ञानं मतं मम ||१३- २ ||

kShetraGYa.n chApi mAM viddhi sarvakShetreShu bhArata .
kShetrakShetraGYayorGYAnaM yattajGYAnaM mataM mama .. 13\-२ ..

kshetraGYaM = the knower of the field; cha = also; api = certainly; maaM = Me; viddhi = know; sarva = all; kshetreshhu = in bodily fields; bhaarata = O son of Bharata; kshetra = the field of activities (the body); kshetraGYayoH = and the knower of the field; GYaanaM = knowledge of; yat.h = that which; tat.h = that; GYaanaM = knowledge; mataM = opinion; mama = My.

Know Me to be the knower of the field for all fields, O Arjuna. The true understanding of both the field and the knower of the field is considered by Me to be the knowledge. (13.02)

तत्क्षेत्रं यच्च यादृक्च यद्विकारि यतश्च यत् |
स च यो यत्प्रभावश्च तत्समासेन मे शृणु ||१३- ३ ||

tatkShetra.n yachcha yAdR^ikcha yadvikAri yatashcha yat.h .

sa cha yo yatprabhAvashcha tatsamAsena me shR^iNu .. 13\-3 ..

tat.h = that; kshetraM = field of activities; yat.h = what; cha = also; yaadR^ik.h = as it is; cha = also; yat.h = having what; vikaari = changes; yataH = from which; cha = also; yat.h = what; saH = he; cha = also; yaH = who; yat.h = having what; prabhaavaH = influence; cha = also; tat.h = that; samaasena = in summary; me = from Me; shR^iNu = understand.

What that Field is and of what nature, how it is transformed, and from where it is, what He is and what His powers are , hear that now briefly from Me. (13.3)

ऋषिभिर्बहुधा गीतं छन्दोभिर्विविधैः पृथक् ।
ब्रह्मसूत्रपदैश्चैव हेतुमद्भिर्विनिश्चितैः ॥१३- ४ ॥

R^iShibhirbahudhA gIta.n chhandobhirvividhaiH pR^ithak.h .

brahmasUtrapadaishchaiva hetumadbhirvinishchitaiH .. 13\-4 ..

R^ishhibhiH = by the wise sages; bahudhaa = in many ways; giitaM = described; chhandobhiH = by Vedic hymns; vividhaiH= various; pR^ithak.h = variously; brahmasuutra = of the Vedanta; padaiH = by the aphorisms; cha = also; eva = certainly; hetumadbhiH = with cause and effect; vinishchitaiH = certain.

The sages have described Him in many ways, in various Vedic hymns, and also in verses of the Brahmasutra full of reasoning. (13.04)

महाभूतान्यहंकारो बुद्धिरव्यक्तमेव च ।
इन्द्रियाणि दशैकं च पञ्च चेन्द्रियगोचराः ॥१३- ५ ॥

mahAbhUtAnyaha.nkAro buddhiravyaktameva cha .

indriyANi dashaika.n cha pa~ncha chendriyagocharAH .. 13\-5 ..

mahaabhuutaanii = the great elements; ahaN^kaaraH = false ego; buddhiH = intelligence; avyaktaM = the unmanifested; eva = certainly; cha = also; indriyaaNi = the senses; dashaikaM = eleven; cha = also; paJNcha = five; cha = also; indriyagocharaaH
= the objects of the senses.

The five great Elements, Individuality, also Reason and the unmanifested, the eleven senses, , and the five pastures of the senses (13.5)

इच्छा द्वेषः सुखं दुःखं संघातश्चेतना धृतिः ।
एतत्क्षेत्रं समासेन सविकारमुदाहृतम् ॥१३- ६ ॥

ichchhA dveShaH sukhaM duHkhaM sa.nghAtashchetanA dhR^itiH .

etatkShetra.n samAsena savikAramudAhR^itam.h .. 13\-6 ..

; ichchhaa = desire; dveshhaH = hatred; sukhaM = happiness; duHkhaM = distress; saN^ghaataH = the aggregate; chetanaa = living symptoms; dhR^itiH = firness; etat.h = all this; kshetraM = the field of activities; samaasena = in summary; savikaaraM = with modifications ; udaahR^itaM = exemplified.

Desire, aversion, pleasure, pain, physical body, intelligence, firmness, these, briefly described, constitute the Field and its modifications. (13.6)

अमानित्वमदम्भित्वमहिंसा क्षान्तिरार्जवम् ।
आचार्योपासनं शौचं स्थैर्यमात्मविनिग्रहः ॥१३- ७ ॥

amAnitvamadambhitvamahi.nsA kShAntirArjavam.h .

AchAryopAsanaM shauchaM sthairyamAtmavinigrahaH .. 13\-7 ..

amaanitvaM = humility; adambhitvaM = pridelessness; ahi.nsaa = nonviolence; kshantiH = tolerance; aarjavaM = simplicity; aachaaryopaasanaM = approaching a bona fide spiritual master; shauchaM = cleanliness; sthairyaM = steadfastness; aatmavinigrahaH = self-control.

Humility, modesty, nonviolence, forbearance, sitting near to the teacher, purity, steadfastness, self-control,(13.7)

इन्द्रियार्थेषु वैराग्यमनहंकार एव च |
जन्ममृत्युजराव्याधिदुःखदोषानुदर्शनम् ||१३- ८ ||

indriyArtheShu vairAgyamanaha.nkAra eva cha .

janmamR^ityujarAvyAdhiduHkhadoShAnudarshanam.h ..

13\-8 ..

indriyaartheshhu = in the matter of the senses; vairaagyaM = renunciation; anahaN^kaaraH = being without false egoism; eva = certainly; cha = also; janma = of birth; mR^ityu = death; jaraa = old age; vyaadhi = and disease; duHkha = of the distress; doshha = the fault; anudarshanaM = observing.

Aversion towards sense objects, absence of ego, constant reflection on the agony and suffering inherent in birth, old age, disease, and death. (13.08)

असक्तिरनभिष्वङ्गः पुत्रदारगृहादिषु |
नित्यं च समचित्तत्वमिष्टानिष्टोपपत्तिषु ||१३- ९ ||

asaktiranabhiShvaN^gaH putradAragR^ihAdiShu .

nitya.n cha samachittatvamiShTAniShTopapattiShu ..

13\-9 ..

asaktiH = being without attachment; anabhishvaN^gaH = being without association; putra = for son; daaraa = wife; gR^ihaadishhu = home, etc.; nityaM = constant; cha = also; samachittatvaM = equilibrium; ishhTa = the desirable; anishhTa = and undesirable; upapattishhu = having obtained.

Detachment, non-attachment with son, wife, and home; unfailing equanimity upon attainment of the desirable and the undesirable; and (13.9)

मयि चानन्ययोगेन भक्तिरव्यभिचारिणी ।
विविक्तदेशसेवित्वमरतिर्जनसंसदि ॥१३- १० ॥

mayi chAnanyayogena bhaktiravyabhichAriNI .

viviktadeshasevitvamaratirjanasa.nsadi .. 13\-10 ..

mayi = unto Me; cha = also; ananyayogena = by unalloyed devotional service; bhaktiH = devotion; avyabhichaariNii = without any break; vivikta = to solitary; desha = places; sevitvaM = aspiring; aratiH = being without attachment; janasa.nsadi = to people in general;

Unswerving devotion to Me by the yoga of exclusivity, love for solitude, distaste for social groups; and (13.10)

अध्यात्मज्ञाननित्यत्वं तत्त्वज्ञानार्थदर्शनम् ।
एतज्ज्ञानमिति प्रोक्तमज्ञानं यदतोऽन्यथा ॥१३- ११ ॥

adhyAtmaGYAnanityatva.n tattvaGYAnArthadarshanam.h

.

etajGYAnamiti proktamaGYAnaM yadato.anyathA .. 13\-

11 ..

adhyaatma = pertaining to the self; GYaana = in knowledge; nityatvaM = constancy; tattvaGYaana = of knowledge of the truth; artha = for the object; darshanaM = philosophy; etat.h = all this; GYaanaM = knowledge; iti = thus; proktaM = declared; aGYaanaM = ignorance; yat.h = that which; ataH = from this; anyathaa = other.

Constancy in the Wisdom of the Self, understanding of the object of essential wisdom ; that is declared to be the Wisdom; all against it is ignorance. (13.11)

ज्ञेयं यत्तत्प्रवक्ष्यामि यज्ज्ञात्वामृतमश्नुते ।
अनादिमत्परं ब्रह्म न सत्तन्नासदुच्यते ॥१३- १२ ॥

GYeyaM yattatpravakShyAmi yajGYAtvAmR^itamashnute

.

anAdimatparaM brahma na sattannAsaduchyate .. 13\-

12..

GYeyaM = the knowable; yat.h = which; tat.h = that; pravakshyaami = I shall now explain; yat.h = which; GYaatvaa =knowing; amR^itaM = nectar; ashnute = one tastes; anaadi = beginningless; matparaM = subordinate to Me; brahma = spirit; na = neither; sat.h = real; tat.h = that; na = nor; asat.h = unreal; uchyate = is said to be.

I will explain that knowledge, knowing which one tastes the nectar of immortality, the beginningless supreme ETERNAL, called neither existant (sat) nor non-existant (asat). (13.12)

सर्वतः पाणिपादं तत्सर्वतोऽक्षिशिरोमुखम् ।
सर्वतः श्रुतिमल्लोके सर्वमावृत्य तिष्ठति ॥१३- १३ ॥

sarvataH pANipAdaM tatsarvato.akShishiromukham.h .

sarvataH shrutimalloke sarvamAvR^itya tiShThati .. 13\-13..

sarvataH = everywhere; paaNi = hands; padaM = legs; tat.h = that; sarvataH = everywhere; akshi = eyes; shiraH = heads; mukhaM = faces; sarvataH = everywhere; shrutimat.h = having ears; loke = in the world; sarvaM = everything; aavR^itya = covering; tishhThati = exists.

Having hands and feet everywhere; having eyes, head, and face everywhere; all-hearing, He dwells in the world, enveloping all.(13.13)

सर्वेन्द्रियगुणाभासं सर्वेन्द्रियविवर्जितम् ।
असक्तं सर्वभृच्चैव निर्गुणं गुणभोक्तृ च ॥१३- १४ ॥

sarvendriyaguNAbhAsaM sarvendriyavivarjitam.h .

asakta.n sarvabhR^ichchaiva nirguNaM guNabhoktR^i cha .. 13\-14 ..

sarva = of all; indriya = senses; guNa = of the qualities; aabhaasaM = the perception; sarva = all; indriya = senses; vivarjitaM = being without; asaktaM = without attachment; sarvabhR^it.h = the maintainer of everyone; cha = also; eva = certainly; nirguNaM = without material qualities; guNabhoktR^i = master of the gunas; cha = also.

He is the perceiver of all sense objects without the senses; unattached, yet the sustainer of all; devoid of the Gunas (qualities), yet the enjoyer of the Gunas (qualities). (13.14)

बहिरन्तश्च भूतानामचरं चरमेव च ।
सूक्ष्मत्वात्तदविज्ञेयं दूरस्थं चान्तिके च तत् ॥१३- १५ ॥

bahirantashcha bhUtAnAmachara.n charameva cha .
sUkShmatvAttadaviGYeyaM dUrastha.n chAntike cha tat.h .. 13\-15..

bahiH = outside; antaH = inside; cha = also; bhuutaanaaM = all that exists; acharaM = not moving(non-living); charaM = moving (living) ; eva = also; cha = and; suukshmatvaat.h = on account of being subtle; tat.h = that; aviGYeyaM = unknowable; duurasthaM = far away; cha = also; antike = near; cha = and; tat.h = that.

He is inside as well as outside all, living and non-living. His subtlety is imperceptible and very near and far away He is. (13.15)

अविभक्तं च भूतेषु विभक्तमिव च स्थितम् ।
भूतभर्तृ च तज्ज्ञेयं ग्रसिष्णु प्रभविष्णु च ॥१३- १६ ॥

avibhakta.n cha bhUteShu vibhaktamiva cha sthitam.h .
bhUtabhartR^i cha tajGYeyaM grasiShNu prabhaviShNu cha .. 13\-16 ..

avibhaktaM = without division; cha = also; bhuuteshhu = in all beings; vibhaktaM = divided; iva = as if; cha = also; sthitaM = situated; bhuutabhartR^i = the maintainer of all living entities; cha = also; tat.h = that; GYeyaM = to be understood
grasishhNu = devouring; prabhavishhNu = prevailing; cha = also.

Undivided, yet appears as if divided in beings; He, the object of knowledge, is the creator, sustainer, and destroyer of (all) beings. (13.16)

ज्योतिषामपि तज्ज्योतिस्तमसः परमुच्यते ।
ज्ञानं ज्ञेयं ज्ञानगम्यं हृदि सर्वस्य विष्ठितम् ॥१३- १७ ॥

jyotiShAmapi tajjyotistamasaH paramuchyate .

GYAnaM GYeyaM GYAnagamya.n hR^idi sarvasya viShThitam.h .. 13\-17 ..

jyotiishhaaM = in all luminous objects; api = also; tat.h = that; jyotiH = the source of light; tamasaH = the darkness; paraM = beyond; uchyate = is said; GYaanaM = knowledge; GYeyaM = to be known; GYaanagamyaM = to be approached by; knowledge; hR^idi = in the heart; sarvasya = of everyone; vishhThitaM = situated.

He, the light of all lights, is said to be beyond darkness. He is the Wisdom, the object of Wisdom, by Wisdom to be reached, seated in the hearts of all. (13.17)

इति क्षेत्रं तथा ज्ञानं ज्ञेयं चोक्तं समासतः |
मद्भक्त एतद्विज्ञाय मद्भावायोपपद्यते ||१३- १८ ||

iti kShetra.n tathA GYAnaM GYeya.n chokta.n samAsataH .

madbhakta etadviGYAya madbhAvAyopapadyate .. 13\-18 ..

iti = thus; kshetraM = the field of activities (the body); tathaa = also; GYaanaM = knowledge; GYeyaM = the knowable; cha = also; uktaM = described; samaasataH = in summary; madbhaktaH = My devotee; etat.h = all this; viGYaaya = after; understanding; madbhaavaaya = to My nature; upapadyate = attains.

Thus the field as well as the knowledge and the object of knowledge have been briefly described. Understanding this, My devotee attains Me. (13.18)

प्रकृतिं पुरुषं चैव विद्ध्यनादी उभावपि |
विकारांश्च गुणांश्चैव विद्धि प्रकृतिसम्भवान् ||१३- १९ ||

prakR^itiM puruSha.n chaiva vid.hdhyanAdI ubhAvapi .

vikArA.nshcha guNA.nshchaiva viddhi prakR^itisambhavAn.h .. 13\-19 ..

prakR^itiM = nature; purushhaM = Brahm or consciousness (Supreme Lord in Samkhya philosophy) ; cha = also; eva = certainly; viddhi = you must know; anaadi = without beginning; ubhau = both; api = also; vikaaraan.h = distortions; cha = also; guNaan.h = the three modes of nature; cha = also; eva = certainly; viddhi = know; prakR^iti = material nature; sambhavaan.h = produced of.

Know that Prakriti (Nature) and Purusha(Consciousness) are both beginningless; and also know that all distortions and Gunas(quality) arise from the Prakriti. (13.19)

कार्यकारणकर्तृत्वे हेतुः प्रकृतिरुच्यते ।
पुरुषः सुखदुःखानां भोक्तृत्वे हेतुरुच्यते ॥१३- २० ॥

kAryakAraNakartR^itve hetuH prakR^itiruchyate .

puruShaH sukhaduHkhAnAM bhoktR^itve heturuchyate .. 13\-20 ..

kaarya = of effect; kaaraNa = and cause; kartR^itve = in the matter of creation; hetuH = the instrument; prakR^itiH = material; nature; uchyate = is said to be; purushhaH = the living entity; sukha = of happiness; duHkhaanaaM = and distress
bhoktR^itve = in enjoyment; hetuH = the instrument; uchyate = is said to be.

The Prakriti (Nature) is said to be the cause of production of physical body and organs (of perception and action). The Purusha (or the consciousness) is said to be the cause of experiencing pleasures and pains. (13.20)

पुरुषः प्रकृतिस्थो हि भुङ्क्ते प्रकृतिजान्गुणान् ।
कारणं गुणसङ्गोऽस्य सदसद्योनिजन्मसु ॥१३- २१ ॥

puruShaH prakR^itistho hi bhuN^.hkte prakR^itijAnguNAn.h .

kAraNaM guNasaN^go.asya sadasadyonijanmasu .. 13\-21 ..

purushhaH = the living entity; prakR^itisthaH = being situated in the material energy; hi = certainly; bhuN^kte = enjoys; prakR^itijaan.h = produced by the material nature; guNaan.h = the modes of nature; karaNaM = the cause; guNasaN^gaH = the association with the modes of nature; asya = of the living entity; sadasat.h = in good and bad; yoni = species of life; janmasu = in births.

The Purusha(consciousness) associating with Prakriti (matter or nature), enjoys the Gunas (qualities) born out of Prakriti (Nature) of Prakriti. Attachment to the Gunas(qualities) is the cause of the birth in good and evil wombs. (13.21)

उपद्रष्टानुमन्ता च भर्ता भोक्ता महेश्वरः |
परमात्मेति चाप्युक्तो देहेऽस्मिन्पुरुषः परः ||१३- २२ ||

upadraShTAnumantA cha bhartA bhoktA maheshvaraH .

paramAtmeti chApyukto dehe.asminpuruShaH paraH .. 13\-22 ..

upadrashhTaa = overseer; anumantaa = permitter; cha = also; bhartaa = who takes care; bhoktaa = supreme enjoyer; maheshvaraH = the Supreme Lord; paramaatma = the Supersoul; iti = also; cha = and; api = indeed; uktaH = is said; dehe = in the body; asmin.h = this; purushhaH = enjoyer; paraH = transcendental.

Observer and permitter, supporter, enjoyer, great Lord and also the supreme Self : thus is said to be in this body the supreme Purusha (Conciousness). (13.22)

य एवं वेत्ति पुरुषं प्रकृतिं च गुणैः सह |
सर्वथा वर्तमानोऽपि न स भूयोऽभिजायते ||१३- २३ ||

ya evaM vetti puruShaM prakR^iti.n cha guNaiH saha .

sarvathA vartamAno.api na sa bhUyo.abhijAyate .. 13\-23 ..

yaH = anyone who; evaM = thus; vetti = understands; purushhaM = the living entity; prakR^itiM = material nature; cha = and

guNaiH = the modes of material nature; saha = with; sarvathaa = in all ways; vartamaanaH = being situated; api = in spite of
na = never; saH = he; bhuuyaH = again; abhijaayate = takes his birth.

He who thus knows the Purusha(conciusness) and Prakriti (Nature) with its Gunas (qualities) , in whatsoever condition he may be, he shall not be born again (13.23)

ध्यानेनात्मनि पश्यन्ति केचिदात्मानमात्मना |
अन्ये साङ्ख्येन योगेन कर्मयोगेन चापरे ||१३- २४ ||

dhyAnenAtmani pashyanti kechidAtmAnamAtmanA .

anye sAN^khyena yogena karmayogena chApare .. 13\-24 ..

dhyaanena = by meditation; aatmani = within the self; pashyanti = see; kechit.h = some; aatmaanaM = in the self; aatmanaa = the self; anye = others; saaN^khyena = of philosophical discussion; yogena = by the yoga system; karmayogeNa = by activities without fruitive desire; cha = also; apare = others.

Some by meditation behold the SELF in the self by the SELF ; others by the Samkhya Yoga, and others by the Yoga of Action. (13.24)

अन्ये त्वेवमजानन्तः श्रुत्वान्येभ्य उपासते |
तेऽपि चातितरन्त्येव मृत्युं श्रुतिपरायणाः ||१३- २५ ||

anye tvevamajAnantaH shrutvAnyebhya upAsate .

te.api chAtitarantyeva mR^ityu.n shrutiparAyaNAH .. 13\-25 ..

anye = others; tu = but; evaM = thus; ajaanantaH = without spiritual knowledge; shrutvaa = by hearing; anyebhyaH = from; others; upaasate = to learn sitting near; te = they; api = also; cha = and; atitaranti = transcend; eva = certainly; mR^ityuM = the path of death; shrutiparaayaNaaH = inclined to the process of hearing.

Others also, ignorant of this, having heard of it from others, begin to worship ; and these also transcend death, believing to what they have heard (13.25)

यावत्सञ्जायते किञ्चित्सत्त्वं स्थावरजङ्गमम् ।
क्षेत्रक्षेत्रज्ञसंयोगात्तद्विद्धि भरतर्षभ ॥१३- २६ ॥

yAvatsa~njAyate ki~nchitsattvaM sthAvarajaN^gamam.h .

kShetrakShetraGYasa.nyogAttadviddhi bharatarShabha ..

13\-26 ..

yaavat.h = whatever; saJNjaayate = comes into being; kiJNchit.h = anything; sattvaM = existence; sthaavara = not moving; jaN^gamaM = moving; kshetra = of the body; kshetraGYa = and the knower of the body; sa.nyogaat.h = by the union between; tadviddhi = you must know it; bharatarshhabha = O chief of the Bharatas.

Whatever is born, moving or not moving, know them to be (born) from the union of the field (or Prakriti) and the field knower (or Purusha), O Arjuna. (13.26)

समं सर्वेषु भूतेषु तिष्ठन्तं परमेश्वरम् ।
विनश्यत्स्वविनश्यन्तं यः पश्यति स पश्यति ॥१३- २७ ॥

samaM sarveShu bhUteShu tiShThantaM parameshvaram.h .

vinashyatsvavinashyanta.n yaH pashyati sa pashyati ..

13\-27 ..

samaM = equally; sarveshhu = in all; bhuuteshhu = living entities; tishhThantaM = residing; parameshvaraM = the Supersoul; vinashyatsu = in the destructible; avinashyantaM = not destroyed; yaH = anyone who; pashyati = sees; saH = he
pashyati = actually sees.

The one who sees the imperishable Supreme Lord dwelling equally within all perishable beings truly sees. (13.27)

समं पश्यन्हि सर्वत्र समवस्थितमीश्वरम् ।
न हिनस्त्यात्मनात्मानं ततो याति परां गतिम् ॥१३- २८ ॥

samaM pashyanhi sarvatra samavasthitamIshvaram.h .

na hinastyAtmanAtmAnaM tato yAti parAM gatim.h .. 13\-28 ..

samaM = equally; pashyan.h = seeing; hi = certainly; sarvatra = everywhere; samavasthitaM = equally situated; iishvaraM = the God; na = does not; hinasti = kills; aatmanaa = by the self; aatmaanaM = to the self; tataH = then; yaati = reaches; paraaM = the transcendental; gatiM = destination.

Seeing indeed everywhere the same Lord equally dwelling, he does not destroy the SELF by the self, and thus treads the highest Path.(13.28)

प्रकृत्यैव च कर्माणि क्रियमाणानि सर्वशः ।
यः पश्यति तथात्मानमकर्तारं स पश्यति ॥१३- २९ ॥

prakR^ityaiva cha karmANi kriyamANAni sarvashaH .

yaH pashyati tathAtmAnamakartAraM sa pashyati .. 13\-29..

prakR^ityaa = by material nature; eva = certainly; cha = also; karmaaNi = activities; kriyamaaNaani = being performed; sarvashaH = in all respects; yaH = anyone who; pashyati = sees; tathaa = also; aatmaanaM = himself; akartaaraM = the nondoer; saH = he; pashyati = sees perfectly.

Those who perceive that all works are done by the (Gunas of) Prakriti alone, and thus they are not the doer, they truly understand. (13.29)

यदा भूतपृथग्भावमेकस्थमनुपश्यति ।
तत एव च विस्तारं ब्रह्म सम्पद्यते तदा ॥१३- ३० ॥

yadA bhUtapR^ithagbhAvamekasthamanupashyati .

tata eva cha vistAraM brahma sampadyate tadA .. 13\-30 ..

yadaa = when; bhuuta = of living entities; pR^ithagbhaavaM = separated identities; ekasthaM = situated in one; anupashyati = one tries to see through authority; tataH eva = thereafter; cha = also; vistaaraM = the expansion; brahma = the Absolute; sampadyate = he attains; tadaa = at that time.

When he perceives the diversified existence of beings as rooted in One, and spreading forth from it, then he reaches the ETERNAL. (13.30)

अनादित्वान्निर्गुणत्वात्परमात्मायमव्ययः ।
शरीरस्थोऽपि कौन्तेय न करोति न लिप्यते ॥१३- ३१ ॥

anAditvAnnirguNatvAtparamAtmAyamavyayaH .

sharIrastho.api kaunteya na karoti na lipyate .. 13\-3१ ..

anaaditvaat.h = due to eternity; nirguNatvaat.h = due to being transcendental; parama = beyond material nature; aatmaa = Self ; ayaM = this; avyayaH = inexhaustible; shariirasthaH = dwelling in the body; api = though; kaunteya = O son of Kunti

na karoti = never does anything; na lipyate = nor is he entangled.

Being beginningless and without qualities, the imperishable supreme SELF, though seated in the body, O Kaunteya, works not nor is affected.(13.31)

यथा सर्वगतं सौक्ष्म्यादाकाशं नोपलिप्यते ।
सर्वत्रावस्थितो देहे तथात्मा नोपलिप्यते ॥१३- ३२ ॥

yathA sarvagataM saukShmyAdAkAshaM nopalipyate .

sarvatrAvasthito dehe tathAtmA nopalipyate .. 13\-32 ..

yathaa = as; sarvagataM = all-pervading; saukshmyaat.h = due to being subtle; aakaashaM = the sky; na = never; upalipyate = mixes; sarvatra = everywhere; avasthitaH = situated; dehe = in the body; tathaa = so; aatmaa = the self; na = never

upalipyate = mixes.

As the all-pervading space is not tainted because of its subtlety, similarly the Self, seated in everybody, is not tainted. (13.32)

यथा प्रकाशयत्येकः कृत्स्नं लोकमिमं रविः ।
क्षेत्रं क्षेत्री तथा कृत्स्नं प्रकाशयति भारत ॥१३- ३३ ॥

yathA prakAshayatyekaH kR^itsna.n lokamimaM raviH .

kShetra.n kShetrI tathA kR^itsnaM prakAshayati bhArata
.. 13\-33 ..

yathaa = as; prakaashayati = illuminates; ekaH = one; kR^itsnaM = the whole; lokaM = universe; imaM = this; raviH = sun; kshetraM = this body; kshetrii = the soul; tathaa = similarly; kR^itsnaM = all; prakaashayati = illuminates; bhaarata = O son of Bharata.

As the one sun illuminates the whole world, so the Lord of the Field illuminates the whole Field, O Bharata.(13.33)

क्षेत्रक्षेत्रज्ञयोरेवमन्तरं ज्ञानचक्षुषा ।
भूतप्रकृतिमोक्षं च ये विदुर्यान्ति ते परम् ॥१३- ३४ ॥

kShetrakShetraGYayorevamantaraM GYAnachakShuShA
.

bhUtaprakR^itimokSha.n cha ye viduryAnti te param.h ..
13\-34 ..

kshetra = of the body; kshetraGYayoH = of the proprietor of the body; evaM = thus; antaraM = the difference; GYaanachakshushhaa = by the vision of knowledge; bhuuta = of the living entity; prakR^iti = from material nature; mokshaM = the liberation; cha = also; ye = those who; viduH = know; yaanti = approach; te = they; paraM = the Supreme.

They who by the eye of Wisdom perceive this difference between the Field and the Knower of the Field, and the liberation of beings from Matter(Nature), they go to the Supreme.(13.34)

ॐ तत्सदिति श्रीमद्भगवद्गीतासूपनिषत्सु
ब्रह्मविद्यायां योगशास्त्रे श्रीकृष्णार्जुनसंवादे
क्षेत्रक्षेत्रज्ञविभागयोगो नाम त्रयोदशोऽध्यायः ॥१३॥

AUM tatsaditi shrImadbhagavadgItAsUpaniShatsu
brahmavidyAyA.n yogashAstre
shrIkR^iShNArjunasa.nvAde
kShetrakShetraGYavibhAgayogo nAma
trayodasho.adhyAyaH .. 13

14. The Nature and its Three Gunas

One God and Father of all, who is over all and through all and in all. ---- Ephesians 4:6

Introduction

Lord unambiguously declares in chapter thirteen that He resides in all beings as their true Self, the real subject of all their senses and feelings, and the one that is responsible for their emotions. The concept is difficult to understand and counterintuitive to general understanding where one believes that God is Supreme and different from an individual being.

Additionally, the concept, while a complex reality, presents a unique difficulty that the Supreme is not accessible to the knowledge senses of an individual, for it is challenging for a subject to observe itself. Like an eye cannot behold itself, the Self cannot gain knowledge regarding itself.

While solving algebra problems we consider as if the unknown quantity is not concealed, but is an alphabetic symbol. Subsequently, with the given relationships, the value of the unknown is straightforward to determine.

As a starting point, one may consider the inner self to be different from the Supreme. Now looking inward, focusing on oneself is no longer required to understand God. He the creator of all, the father of all beings is evident in all his creation. You also the part of it.

The way of approaching the Supreme in this way, where considering oneself as part of the Supreme is called bhakti-yoga in Bhagavad-Gita. Bhakt is a Sanskrit word meaning "forming part of". Bhaktas, therefore, consider themselves as part of the Supreme.

Presenting the method to achieve the abode of the Supreme through bhakti-yoga and merge into Him, Lord describes the Prakriti born from the Supreme. Produced from the Prakriti, the three Gunas are responsible for the delusion of the beings. Going beyond the three Gunas is the way to overcome the delusion and to merge back into the Supreme.

Chapter Summary

The sublime knowledge described in this chapter has liberated the sages from the bondage of the world, declares Lord Krishna. After gaining this knowledge, the beings are neither born in the creation nor disturbed in the dissolution. The previous chapter describes the cause of the world as the union between Nature and Spirit (Prakriti and Purusha). Here Lord says that the creation emerges from his womb symbolised as Brahma, and He germinates it.
He, therefore, is the Father of all beings.

Nature, the material cause of all beings demonstrates three Guna or qualities: Sattva, Rajas and Tamas. Originating from Prakriti, the three Gunas shackle the creatures, separating them from the Supreme. Of these, the Sattva, from its stainlessness, is harmonious and healthy, binds by attachment to happiness and knowledge. Rajas, on the other hand, having the qualities of passion and craving, ties the subjects by attachment to action. Further, Tamas, the property of dullness originates from ignorance and deludes them, fastening by heedlessness and indolence.

All the three Gunas bind the subject through attachment, Sattva attaches to happiness, Rajas to action, while Tamas, enshrouding wisdom, attaches, to heedlessness. With the predominance of the Sattva, the subject finds itself inclined towards the light of knowledge. Greed, activity, the undertaking of works, unrest, and desire arise when Rajas is predominant. Darkness, inactivity, negligence and delusion increase, when Tamas increases.

If Sattva prevails when the embodied goes to dissolution, then he goes forth to the spotless worlds of the great Sages. Demising during the predominance of Rajas, the subject is born among those attached to action. Contrarily, if dissolved in Tamas, he is born in the wombs of the foolish.

In summary, the fruit of Sattva is harmony and happiness, the outcome of Rajas is pain, and the result of Tamas is unwisdom. Settled in Sattva, beings rise upward, in Rajas, they dwell in the midmost place. Enveloped in the vilest qualities, those lodged in Tamas go downward.

Perceiving no agent acting other than the three Gunas (sattva, rajas tams) and knowing Him who is beyond the Gunas, one attains the abode of the Supreme. Having crossed beyond these three Gunas, which are the source of the body, the subject realises its true Self and is freed· from birth, death, decay and pain, and attains, the immortal state.

Listening that the wise man goes beyond the Gunas, while still alive and attains the eternal state of the Supreme, Arjuna curiously asked Lord about the marks and conduct of such a person. He also asks about his ways to pass beyond the three Gunas.

Lord replied that such a person neither hates the effects of three Gunas such as light, activity, and delusion, nor longs for them. About the conduct of such a person, Lord responded that seated as neutral, thinking that the Gunas act, he is not moved by the Gunas. To him, pain and pleasure are alike, a clod of stone and a piece of gold are similar, friends and foes are equal. That man of wisdom considers praise and censure as same. Having abandoned all undertakings, he, who has crossed beyond the Gunas, remains equanimous in honour and disgrace and behaves the same with friends and enemies.

Thinking oneself without straying as part of the Eternal Supreme as explained in this discourse of bhakti-yoga, one easily crosses beyond the Gunas of the Prakriti and is fit to become the Eternal. For Supreme Self is the indestructible nectar of immortality, perennial righteousness, and perpetual bliss.

Analysis:

Introduction:

Lord Krishna declares that the sublime knowledge, which he is again going to reveal is the best as it has resulted in the salvation of many sages. The Lord then proclaims that this doctrine is the sure path to perfection. Knowing this, one manages to conquer the agony of life and death in the universe. Lord says that those who resort to this knowledge, attaining similarity with the nature of Supreme, do not take rebirth at the time of creation, nor are they disturbed in cataclysm.

Here some words are notable, the use of the phrase "again going to reveal " and the use of epithet "best" and "sublime" before the knowledge which he is going to reveal.

Lord Krishna emphasising that he is again going to reveal the knowledge, implies that he has already professed the wisdom declared here. However, Gita is a concise treatise (700 verses) of eternal wisdom, then why Lord will retell the same doctrine. Either the viewpoint to express the same truth is different, or the matter is so significant that he considers it imperative enough to re-emphasise in other words.

Further exploration of the chapter indicates that Lord explains the concept here from a different perspective. Further, Lord praises the knowledge that he is going to profess, by the epithet "sublime" and "best" to arouse curiosity in the minds of the listeners.

As explained in the analysis section of chapter 13, the cause of rebirth is the causal body, formed at the time of death due to Nescience (Avidya). The reason for the causal body, the Avidya is destroyed by the preachings that the Lord teaches here. The subject understanding this does not take rebirth at the time of creation, therefore. For she obtains stability of the mind, she is also not disturbed at the time of the cataclysm.

Supreme as the Father and Mother of All:

in the next two verses, Lord says I am the womb of all creatures, and I plant the seed in the universal womb, I am, therefore, also the father of all beings.

Womb here poetically represents Prakriti (nature), which is the material cause of the universe. Here

Prakriti, originating from Supreme is Brahma, the material cause of all beings and Supreme the father of all implants seeds in Prakriti.

The Supreme Lord has two potencies--the Prakriti or the Kshetra, and the Purusha or Khetragya as described in chapter 13. It is the union of Prakriti with the Purusha which creates the Golden womb (Hiranyagarbha), the conditions ripe for the creation of all beings. It might have inspired the concept of Lord Shiva in the form of ***Ardhnarishwar*** , the God in the form of half male and half female. Avidya (nescience), kama (desire) and karma (action) play a vital role in this process. Being the material in sublime clause of all the creatures, Lord is father and mother of all beings.

The Three Gunas Model of Prakriti:

Lord Krishna says that the three Gunas (qualities), namely Sattva, Rajas and Tamas originate from the Prakriti. These three Gunas bind the imperishable self in the bodies of the beings. Guna here is a technical term, and interpreting it as property, quality, or attribute is a simplistic translation. Guna like quality does not imply independent existence of an attribute and substance, as in case of shape and object. Accordingly, the Gunas, like the attributes of an item, ever depends on another the pure consciousness, as they are only forms of avidya or nescience. Self, as pure consciousness, on the other hand, is without any attributes as explained already. Born out of Lord's Maya (nescience), the Gunas bind fast the embodied.

In chapter 13.31, Lord has proclaimed that SELF remains untainted, then now, on the contrary, Lord says here that Gunas bind him fast? The philosophy explained in chapter 13 considers Supreme residing into all beings as their imperishable SELF. However, it becomes quite complex to understand by commoners, as the discrimination between the ego, and the true SELF is not straightforward. The ego, produced through rajas makes them act with the idea that they are the doer, while SELF is pure consciousness, the Supreme, that just observes their acts, and enable them to have emotions and feelings.

To enlighten the people who cannot understand the nuances of the higher-order wisdom explained earlier, Lord proceeds without discrimination between "self" and "ego". He continues with the idea that the "self" is the concept which people regard as the real agent of their acts. It is the one that resides in their bodies and is responsible for their feelings and consciousness. Thus it is also called ***dehi*** (a Sanskrit word), the one, which lives in the body.

For simplicity, let us assume that the Supreme Lord is the universal consciousness, while the self of a being or ***dehi*** is the consciousness of the creature. Let individual dehi, having similar attributes as that of the Supreme, be the part of the whole Supreme.

Now, as per the assumption that the dehi is the agent of actions, the actions of a Dehi should bind him to his acts. Lord therefore declares, the three Gunas, Satva, Rajas and Tamas, bind down in the body, O Arjuna, the imperishable dehi, the self. The declaration appears to be contrary to those elaborated earlier where the Self is considered untaintable, because of the present simplistic start point.

Shruti (Upanishads), however, says that the Supreme resides in the heart of every being in the form of their self. Lord has also reiterated the point at many places in the Bhagwat Gita. Brahadaranyak Upanishad says:

ॐ पूर्णमदः पूर्णमिदं पूर्णात्पूर्णमुदच्यते ।
पूर्णस्य पूर्णमादाय पूर्णमेवावशिष्यते ॥

Meaning of the shloka is "That (Supreme eternal) is complete and infinite, and so is This (the self in the beings). This Complete (self) emerges from That complete (Eternal Supreme). Deducting This (self) from That (the Supreme Eternal) , it (Supreme Eternal) still remains complete and infinite.

The Infinite Supreme is the cause of the origin of all beings. Their self is the fraction of the Supreme. Now let us analyse this concept from the point of view of mathematics. Mathematically, a finite fraction of an infinite quantity is also infinite, and the original quantity still remains infinite. It implies that when the finite number of self of beings are created from the Supreme Infinite, then each self thus created is also infinite having same properties as of Supreme. Further, even after creating many such beings, the Supreme still remains infinite. Therefore theoretically speaking, having the same infinite consciousness in all beings is similar to having the parts of that infinite supreme in all beings.

The principles of Bhakti Yoga, where the self of the beings are considered as part of the Supreme, theoretically leads to the same conclusions as the principles of Gyan yoga, where the same Supreme is said to be residing in all beings as their inner Self.

The Three Gunas:

How the inner self interplays with the material bodies of the beings, what are the attributes of the material body? How are they important to know the characteristics and behaviour of the creatures become clear if we understand the Prakriti, and its tendencies, which define the material existence.

The Gunas are the three tendencies of the Prakrti or the three strands forming the twisted rope of nature. Sattva represents the light of consciousness and is irradiated by it, and therefore has the quality of radiance. Restlessness for action is the characteristics of Rajasa, Heedlessness and indifference emanate from Tamas.

Of these, Sattva being unadulterated causes illumination and health, but binds with attachment to happiness and knowledge. Knowledge here is not the wisdom of the Supreme but the lower level learning of worldly things. Sattva does not liberate from the sense of ego. It also creates desire, though of noble elements, and therefore binds.

Rajasa is of the nature of passion, from which arises thirst and attachment. Craving for what has not been attained and fondness to what has been achieved. Rajasa binds fast the embodied Self by attachment to action. The third Guna, Tamasa, is born of ignorance and causes delusion or non-discrimination in all embodied beings.

Sattva attaches to happiness, Rajas to action, while Tamas, clouding the wisdom, fastens to the heedlessness. Enshrouding as veil, covering the judgment caused by Sattva, Tamas attaches to heedlessness and leads to non-performance of necessary duties.

Mutual Action and Predominance of Gunas:

How the Gunas interplay amongst themselves and when the subject exhibits the tendencies related to which Guna?

Lord clarifies that when the Sattva increases, prevailing over Rajasa and Tamasa, then, asserting itself, Sattva produces its effects, knowledge and happiness. Similarly, when the Rajasa dominates over Tamasa and Sattva, then it increases restlessness and desire to act. When Tamasa guna increases, preponderating over Rajasa and Sattva, it produces effects such as eclipsing the wisdom and heedlessness.

Describing the effects of the predominance of Gunas in a body, Lord says, when the Sattva prevails, wisdom light shoots up in every gate of the body. Every sense acts as a gateway of perception for the subject.

When the light of knowledge springs up from every sense organ, it indicates that the Sattva is increasing and predominating. Growing greed, activity, the undertaking of actions, restlessness and craving are signs that the Rajasa guna is on the rise. Absence of discrimination, extreme inactivity, heedlessness and delusion, these are the marks of a person with increasing Tamasa Guna.

Effect of Gunas at the time of Death:

As explained, attachment and desires are all due to Gunas. They also influence the results after the demise of the physical body. When the dissolution takes place during the predominance of sattva, the subject is born among the sages.

Extinction of the physical body while the Rajasa Guna is on the rise, the subject takes birth amongst the people who are attached to action. Whereas, dying at the time when Tamasa Guna is ascending, the person is born amongst irrationals.

Summary of Effect of Guna:

The fruit of good action is Sattvik and pure, that leads to wisdom. The outcome of Rajasa is pain and restlessness that produces greed. Tamasa brings heedlessness and delusion, leading to ignorance. Those who follow sattva go upward, followers of Rajasa remain in the middle and dominated by Tamasa go down.

Importance of going beyond Guna:

In the preceding sections, the Lord has taught us about the cause of the universe -- the apparent birth of Purusha in the womb of high and low creatures. It appears that the Self, under the influence of illusionary knowledge, identifies himself with the Prakriti, longing for the objects of experience. Under the spell of Guna, he feels that he is happy, sorrowful or deluded. Lord has described in detail here, how the Gunas bind the Self due to nescience? The Self here is not the real Self, the Supreme, but the one which is created by illusionary knowledge or nescience.

Going beyond the Gunas to get Immortality:

Now to emphasise that Moksha accrues from the real knowledge, Lord says that when the seer beholds no other agent except the Gunas and knows Him who is higher than the Gunas, he attains the being of the Supreme. Enlightened to realise that there is no agent other than the Gunas which transform themselves into the bodies, senses, and sense-objects, when he sees that it is the Gunas and their modifications acting as the agent in all actions; when he beholds the real Self, who is distinct from the Gunas, who is the mere Witness of them and their functions, then he attains to the being of the Supreme.

The wise man crosses, while still alive, beyond the three Gunas evolved out of nescience. The nescience projects the world and the illusionary Self, which appears real. With the discriminatory knowledge, he becomes free from dissolution, birth, pleasure and pain attaining immortality and in this way accomplishing the being of the supreme.

Listening that a wise person can traverse beyond the Gunas and attain immortality, Arjun found it appropriate to ask the signs and conduct of a such a person, and also how he crosses beyond the three Gunas.

Lord replied that such a person does not abominate illumination, activity and delusion when they arise nor longs for them when they cease.

When Sattva, Rajasa or Tamas Guna arise, the person knows it from an increase in light of wisdom, greed or delusion respectively. Even knowing fully that these Gunas bind him through attachment, a wise person does not hate them. Nor does he long for such Gunas on their disappearance due to his non-attachment. The mark elaborated here serves for self-assessment only, as no other person can perceive the hatred or desire going on in another person's mind.

Answering to the question of the conduct of a wise person, Lord says, such a person remains neutral, not deviating by the Gunas and thinking that Gunas act, while the self is a mere observer. He considers pleasure and pain, friends and foe, and a clod of earth, stone and gold alike. For such a person of wisdom, condemnation and commendation are also same. He remains unaffected thinking that the Gunas transforming themselves into the body, senses, and sense objects act and react upon each other.

Abandoning all undertaking, equanimous in honour and disgrace, and the same towards friends and enemies, he is said to have crossed beyond the Gunas.

Answering the next part of the question, that how one crosses beyond the three Gunas, Lord says that the one who considers his self as a part of the Supreme(Bhakti yoga), practising this, he becomes one with Him. For, He, the Supreme Self is indestructible nectar of immortality, eternal Dharma, and never-ending bliss.

A reference to bhakti-yoga comes here, which is often translated as the yoga of devotion towards the Supreme God. However, as explained before, it may be noted that Lord in Gita has not discussed devotion as a means to attain the Supreme. Devotion is a much later concept but the foundation of devotion may lie in the Bhakti Yoga defined in the Gita. Bhakti here conveys the meaning of considering oneself as part of the Supreme.

With the conviction that the individual Self is a part of the Supreme who is eternal, formless, and without any qualities, one naturally visualises their internal Self also having the same attributes. Like the Supreme, being omnipresent and always observing the creatures indulging in acts, the individual Self also behaves as an observer only and does not act.

Considering individual Self different from the Supreme Self makes it easier to understand the supreme as an observer and then apply the same attributes to oneself as part of Him. On the other hand, considering Supreme as your true Self presents a difficulty in understanding the Supreme, for a subject cannot observe itself.

The three Guna model, which Lord has described here resolves the issue of the real agents of actions of the beings if their selves are just observers. With no distinction between the true Self and that created by false knowledge, it is essential to get rid of the idea of agency in all acts. According to the Three Guna model, the Gunas only act, and the idea, that I am the doer is avoided, thus eliminating ego.

Summary of discussion:

Bhagvat Gita and the Upanishads describe God as supreme consciousness residing in all beings, which is also responsible for their subjective experiences such as beholding, listening etc. The real characteristics of God are that He has no attributes. God is formless, shapeless, unborn and eternal, for He is beyond space and time concept which define the spatial and temporal characteristics defining all traits. He is Sat or the only reality creating space-time world through the interplay of senses and the consciousness. The world appearing real is, on the other hand, unreal because it is a mere illusion created by the interaction of sense organs and awareness. He is also conscious and blissful, for He is beyond attachment to things or experiences. Non-attachment does not disturb His joyous state. Real (Sat), conscious (Chitt), and bliss (Ananda) are his attributes if they can be defined so.

Philosophers define this concept as Advaita or non-dualism. The idea of Advaita presents some challenges to human understanding because of the following reasons.

1. God is a formless, eternal and omnipresent entity. As we do not come across any such objects in our experience, the concept is complex to grasp.
2. God resides in all beings as their consciousness, which understands, receives, and interprets sensual inputs. He is the subject of all experiences in creatures. Like the eye cannot see itself similarly, the beings are blind towards their true self, the Supreme.

Introduction of the duality between God and the individual solves the above two issues. If God and self are two distinct entities, then it is easier for a person to imagine Him. Symbolically one can imagine God as other familiar formless concepts such as light or sound. Ved and Vedant define Om, a monosyllable sound as a symbolic representation of God. As a result of the introduction of duality, the object of understanding, God, is different from the subject who wishes to understand Him.

In Bhakti-Yoga, the conscious existence of a subject is part of God, the Supreme, and its physical reality is part of Prakriti, consisting of three Gunas -- Sattva, Rajasa and Tamasa.

The three Gunas bind the subject to its fruit of action, where the acts are performed under the influence of Sattva, Rajasa, or Tamasa Guna. The Gunas create an attachment to the fruit of action and also generate a sense of doership. This false sense of doership is nescience and the reason of entanglement in the world. If the subject goes beyond the Gunas, thinking that the Gunas only act, and the idea, that I am the doer is avoided, he is able to eliminate the ego. Thus the subject becomes one with the Supreme, observing just the acts without having any idea of agency.

A reference to bhakti-yoga comes here, which is often translated as the yoga of devotion towards the Supreme God. However, as explained before, it may be noted that Lord in Gita has not discussed devotion as a means to attain the Supreme. Bhakti here conveys the meaning of considering oneself as part of the Supreme.

With the conviction that the individual Self is a part of the Supreme who is eternal, formless, and without any qualities, one naturally visualises their internal Self also having the same attributes. Like the Supreme, being omnipresent and always observing the creatures indulging in acts, the individual Self also behaves as an observer only and does not act.

Considering individual Self different from the Supreme Self makes it easier to understand the supreme as an observer and then apply the same attributes to oneself as part of Him. On the other hand, considering Supreme as your true Self presents a difficulty in understanding the Supreme, for a subject cannot observe itself.

The three Guna model, which Lord has described here resolves the issue of the real agents of actions of the beings if their selves are just observers. With no distinction between the true Self and that created by false knowledge, it is essential to get rid of the idea of agency in all acts to get free from the consequences of actions. According to the Three Guna model, the Gunas only act, and the concept that "I am the doer" is avoided, thus eliminating ego and setting one free from the bonds of fruit of actions.

Original Sanskrit with Word Meanings, Transliteration and Translation (Chapter-14)

अथ चतुर्दशोऽध्यायः । गुणत्रयविभागयोगः

atha chaturdasho.adhyAyaH . guNatrayavibhAgayogaH
shrIbhagavAnuvAcha .
Here begins the fourteenth chapter
(guNatrayavibhAgayogaH)

श्रीभगवानुवाच ।
परं भूयः प्रवक्ष्यामि ज्ञानानां ज्ञानमुत्तमम् ।
यज्ज्ञात्वा मुनयः सर्वे परां सिद्धिमितो गताः ॥१४- १॥

paraM bhUyaH pravakShyAmi GYAnAnA.n GYAnamuttamam.h
yajGYAtvA munayaH sarve parAM siddhimito gatAH .. 14\-1..

shriibhagavaanuvaacha = the Supreme Lord ; paraM = highest ; bhuuyaH = again; pravakshyaami = I shall speak; GYaanaanaaM = of all knowledge; GYaanaM = knowledge; uttamaM = the supreme; yat.h = which; GYaatvaa = knowing; munayaH = the sages; sarve = all; paraM = highest ; siddhiM = perfection; itaH = from this world; gataaH = attained.

The Supreme Lord said: I shall further explain to you that supreme knowledge, the best of all knowledge, knowing that all the sages have attained supreme perfection after this life. (14.01)

इदं ज्ञानमुपाश्रित्य मम साधर्म्यमागताः ।
सर्गेऽपि नोपजायन्ते प्रलये न व्यथन्ति च ॥१४- २॥

idaM GYAnamupAshritya mama sAdharmyamAgatAH .
sarge.api nopajAyante pralaye na vyathanti cha .. 14\-2..

idaM = this; GYaanaM = knowledge; upaashritya = taking shelter of; mama = My; saadharmyaM = similar nature; aagataH = having attained;

sarge.api = even in the creation; na = never; upajaayante = are born; pralaye = in the annihilation; na = nor; vyathanti = are disturbed; cha = also.

Those who have taken refuge in this knowledge attain similarity with my nature, and are neither born at the time of creation nor afflicted at the time of dissolution. (14.02)

मम योनिर्महद्ब्रह्म तस्मिन्गर्भं दधाम्यहम् ।

सम्भवः सर्वभूतानां ततो भवति भारत ॥१४- ३॥

mama yonirmahad.h brahma tasmingarbha.n dadhAmyaham.h .

sambhavaH sarvabhUtAnA.n tato bhavati bhArata .. 14\-3..

mama = My; yoniH = source of birth; mahat.h = great; brahma = supreme, eternal; tasmin.h = in that; garbhaM = germinate; dadhaami = create; ahaM = I; sambhavaH = the possibility; sarvabhuutaanaaM = of all living entities; tataH = thereafter; bhavati = becomes; bhaarata = O son of Bharata.

My womb is the great ETERNAL; in that I place the germ ; from there originate all beings, O Bharata. (14.03)

सर्वयोनिषु कौन्तेय मूर्तयः सम्भवन्ति याः ।

तासां ब्रह्म महद्योनिरहं बीजप्रदः पिता ॥१४- ४॥

sarvayoniShu kaunteya mUrtayaH sambhavanti yAH .

tAsAM brahma mahadyoniraham bIjapradaH pitA .. 14\-4..

sarvayonishhu = in all species of life; kaunteya = O son of Kunti; muurtayaH = mortals; sambhavanti = they appear; yaH = which; taasaaM = of all of them; brahma = the supreme; mahadyoniH = great womb; ahaM = I; biijapradaH = the seed-giving; pitaa = father.

In whatsoever wombs mortals are produced. O Kaunteya, the ETERNAL is their mighty womb, I the ETERNAL, their generating father. (14.4)

सत्त्वं रजस्तम इति गुणाः प्रकृतिसम्भवाः ।

निबध्नन्ति महाबाहो देहे देहिनमव्ययम् ॥१४- ५॥

sattvaM rajastama iti guNAH prakR^itisambhavAH .

nibadhnanti mahAbAho dehe dehinamavyayam.h .. 14\-5..

sattvaM = the mode of goodness; rajaH = the mode of passion; tamaH = the mode of ignorance; iti = thus; guNaaH = the qualities; prakR^iti = material nature; sambhavaaH = produced of; nibadhnanti = do condition; mahaabaaho = O mighty-armed one; dehe = in this body; dehiinaM = the living entity; avyayaM = eternal.

Sattva or harmony, Rajas or activity, and Tamas or inertia; these three Gunas (qualities) are matter born. They bind fast in the body, O great armed one, the imperishable dweller in the body. (14.05)

तत्र सत्त्वं निर्मलत्वात्प्रकाशकमनामयम् ।
सुखसङ्गेन बध्नाति ज्ञानसङ्गेन चानघ ॥१४- ६॥

tatra sattvaM nirmalatvAtprakAshakamanAmayam.h .
sukhasaN^gena badhnAti GYAnasaN^gena chAnagha .. 14\-6..

tatra = there; sattvaM = the mode of goodness; nirmalatvaat.h = being purest in the material world; prakaashakaM = illuminating; anaamayaM = without any sinful reaction; sukha = with happiness; saN^gena = by association; badhnaati = binds; GYaana = with knowledge; saN^gena = attachment; cha = also; anagha = O sinless one.

Of these Harmony (satva), through its stainlessness, luminous and healthy properties, binds by the attachment to bliss and the attachment to wisdom, O sinless one. (14.06)

रजो रागात्मकं विद्धि तृष्णासङ्गसमुद्भवम् ।
तन्निबध्नाति कौन्तेय कर्मसङ्गेन देहिनम् ॥१४- ७॥

rajo rAgAtmakaM viddhi tR^iShNAsaN^gasamudbhavam.h .
tannibadhnAti kaunteya karmasaN^gena dehinam.h .. 14\-7.

rajaH = the mode of passion; raagaatmakaM = born of desire or lust; viddhi = know; tR^ishhNaa = with hankering; saN^ga = association; samudbhavaM = produced of; tat.h = that; nibadhnaati = binds; kaunteya = O son of Kunti; karmasaN^gena = by association with fruitive activity; dehinaM = the embodied (beings).

The passion-nature (rajao guna), know that, is the source of attachment and thirst for life, O Kaunteya, that binds the embodied by the attachment to action. (14.07)

तमस्त्वज्ञानजं विद्धि मोहनं सर्वदेहिनाम् ।
प्रमादालस्यनिद्राभिस्तन्निबध्नाति भारत ॥१४- ८॥

tamastvaGYAnajaM viddhi mohanaM sarvadehinAm.h .
pramAdAlasyanidrAbhistannibadhnAti bhArata .. 14\-8..

tamaH = the mode of ignorance; tu = but; aGYaanajaM = produced of ignorance; viddhi = know; mohanaM = the delusion; sarvadehinaaM = of all embodied beings; pramaada = with madness; alasya = indolence; nidraabhiH = and sleep; tat.h = that; nibadhnaati = binds; bhaarata = O son of Bharata.

But Inertia (Tamas), know that, born of un-wisdom, is the deluder of all embodied beings; that binds by heedlessness, indolence and sloth, O Bharata. (14.08)

सत्त्वं सुखे सञ्जयति रजः कर्मणि भारत ।

ज्ञानमावृत्य तु तमः प्रमादे सञ्जयत्युत ॥१४- ९॥

sattvaM sukhe sa~njayati rajaH karmaNi bhArata .
GYAnamAvR^itya tu tamaH pramAde sa~njayatyuta .. 14\-9..

sattvaM = the mode of goodness; sukhe = in happiness; saJNjayati = binds; rajaH = the mode of passion; karmaaNi = in fruitive activity; bhaarata = O son of Bharata; GYaanaM = knowledge; aavR^itya = covering; tu = but; tamaH = the mode of ignorance; pramaade = in madness; saJNjayati = binds; uta = it is said.

Sattva attaches to bliss, Rajas to action, O Bharata! By shrouding knowledge, however, Tamas attaches to heedlessness. (14.09)

रजस्तमश्चाभिभूय सत्त्वं भवति भारत ।

रजः सत्त्वं तमश्चैव तमः सत्त्वं रजस्तथा ॥१४- १०॥

rajastamashchAbhibhUya sattvaM bhavati bhArata .
rajaH sattvaM tamashchaiva tamaH sattvaM rajastathA .. 14\-10..

rajaH = the mode of passion; tamaH = the mode of ignorance; cha = also; abhibhuuya = surpassing; sattvaM = the mode of goodness; bhavati = becomes prominent; bhaarata = O son of Bharata; rajaH = the mode of passion; sattvaM = the mode of goodness; tamaH = the mode of ignorance; cha = also; eva = like that; tamaH = the mode of ignorance; sattvaM = the mode of goodness; rajaH = the mode of passion; tathaa = thus.

Sattva dominates by suppressing Rajas and Tamas, O Bharat; Rajas by suppressing Sattva and Tamas; and Tamas by suppressing Sattva and Rajas, O Arjuna. (14.10)

सर्वद्वारेषु देहेऽस्मिन्प्रकाश उपजायते ।

ज्ञानं यदा तदा विद्याद्विवृद्धं सत्त्वमित्युत ॥१४- ११॥

sarvadvAreShu dehe.asminprakAsha upajAyate .
GYAnaM yadA tadA vidyAdvivR^iddha.n sattvamityuta .. 14\-11..

sarvadvaareshhu = in all the gates; dehe.asmin.h = in this body; prakaashaH = the quality of illumination; upajaayate = develops; GYaanaM = knowledge; yadaa = when; tadaa = at that time; vidyaat.h = know;

vivR^iddhaM = increased; sattvaM = the mode of goodness; ityuta = thus it is said.

When the wisdom light enters through all the gates of the body, then it should be known that Sattva is predominant.(14.11)

लोभः प्रवृत्तिरारम्भः कर्मणामशमः स्पृहा।

रजस्येतानि जायन्ते विवृद्धे भरतर्षभ ||१४- १२||

lobhaH pravR^ittirArambhaH karmaNAmashamaH spR^ihA .

rajasyetAni jAyante vivR^iddhe bharatarShabha .. 14\-12..

lobhaH = greed; pravR^ittiH = activity; aarambhaH = endeavour; karmaNaaM = in activities; ashamaH = uncontrollable; spR^ihaa = desire; rajasi = Rajo Guna (mobility); etaani = all these; jaayante = develop; vivR^iddhe = when there is an excess; bharatarshhabha = O chief of the descendants of Bharata.

Greed, outgoing energy, undertaking of actions, restlessness, desire these are born of the increase of Rajas (Mobility) , O best of the Bharatas. (14.12)

अप्रकाशोऽप्रवृत्तिश्च प्रमादो मोह एव च।

तमस्येतानि जायन्ते विवृद्धे कुरुनन्दन ||१४- १३||

aprakAsho.apravR^ittishcha pramAdo moha eva cha .

tamasyetAni jAyante vivR^iddhe kurunandana .. 14\-13..

aprakaashaH = darkness; apravR^ittiH = inactivity; cha = and; pramaadaH = heedlessness; mohaH = illusion; eva = certainly; cha = also; tamasi = the mode of ignorance; etaani = these; jaayante = are manifested; vivR^iddhe = when developed; kurunandana = O son of Kuru.

Darkness, stagnation and heedlessness and also delusion these are born of the increase of Inertia, O joy of the Kurus. (14.13)

यदा सत्त्वे प्रवृद्धे तु प्रलयं याति देहभृत्।

तदोत्तमविदां लोकानमलान्प्रतिपद्यते ||१४- १४||

yadA sattve pravR^iddhe tu pralayaM yAti dehabhR^it.h .

tadottamavidA.n lokAnamalAnpratipadyate .. 14\-14..

yadaa = when; sattve = the mode of goodness; pravR^iddhe = developed; tu = but; pralayaM = dissolution; yaati = goes; dehabhR^it.h = the embodied; tadaa = at that time; uttamavidaaM = of the great sages; lokaan.h = the planets; amalaan.h = pure; pratipadyate = attains.

If Harmony verily prevails when the embodied goes to dissolution, then he goes forth to the spotless worlds of the great Sages. (14.14)

रजसि प्रलयं गत्वा कर्मसङ्गिषु जायते ।
तथा प्रलीनस्तमसि मूढयोनिषु जायते ॥१४- १५॥
rajasi pralayaM gatvA karmasaN^giShu jAyate .
tathA pralInastamasi mUDhayoniShu jAyate .. 14\-15..

rajasi = in passion; pralayaM = dissolution; gatvaa = attaining; karmasaN^gishhu = in the association of those engaged in fruitive activities; jaayate = takes birth; tathaa = similarly; praliinaH = being dissolved; tamasi = in ignorance; muuDhayonishhu = in animal species; jaayate = takes birth.

Having gone to dissolution in Mobility(rajas), he is born among those attached to action ; if dissolved in Inertia(tamas), he is born in the wombs of the foolish. (14.15)

कर्मणः सुकृतस्याहुः सात्त्विकं निर्मलं फलम् ।
रजसस्तु फलं दुःखमज्ञानं तमसः फलम् ॥१४- १६॥
karmaNaH sukR^itasyAhuH sAttvikaM nirmalaM phalam.h .
rajasastu phalaM duHkhamaGYAnaM tamasaH phalam.h .. 14\-16..

karmaNaH = of work; sukR^itasya = pious action; aahuH = is said; saattvikaM = harmonious qualities (satvik); nirmalaM = purified; phalaM = the result; rajasaH = quality of action and passion; tu = but; phalaM = the result; duHkhaM = misery; aGYaanaM = ignorance; tamasaH = quality of inertia; phalaM = the result.

The fruit of good action is said to be harmonious qualities (Saattvika) and pure, the fruit of quality of mobility (Raajasika action) is pain, and the fruit of inertia (Taamasika action) is ignorance. (14.16)

सत्त्वात्सञ्जायते ज्ञानं रजसो लोभ एव च ।
प्रमादमोहौ तमसो भवतोऽज्ञानमेव च ॥१४- १७॥
sattvAtsa~njAyate GYAnaM rajaso lobha eva cha .
pramAdamohau tamaso bhavato.aGYAnameva cha .. 14\-17..

sattvaat.h = from the qualities of goodness; saJNjaayate = develops; GYaanaM = knowledge; rajasaH = from the qualities of passion; lobhaH = greed; eva = certainly; cha = also; pramaada = madness; mohau = and illusion; tamasaH = from the qualities of ignorance; havataH = develop; aGYaanaM = nonsense; eva = certainly; cha = also.

Knowledge arises from Sattva; desires arise from Rajas; and negligence, delusion, and ignorance arise from Tamas. (14.17)

ऊर्ध्वं गच्छन्ति सत्त्वस्था मध्ये तिष्ठन्ति राजसाः ।
जघन्यगुणवृत्तिस्था अधो गच्छन्ति तामसाः ॥१४- १८॥

Urdhva.n gachchhanti sattvasthA madhye tiShThanti rAjasAH .
jaghanyaguNavR^ittisthA adho gachchhanti tAmasAH .. 14\-18..

uurdhvaM = upwards; gachchhanti = go; sattvasthaaH = those situated in the mode of goodness; madhye = in the middle; tishhThanti = dwell; raajasaaH = those situated in the mode of passion; jaghanya = of abominable; guNa = quality; vR^ittisthaaH = whose occupation; adhaH = down; gachchhanti = go; taamasaaH = persons in the mode of ignorance.

They rise upwards who are settled in Harmony(sattva) ; the Active(rajasik) dwell in the midmost place ; the Inert (tamasik) go downwards, enveloped in the vilest qualities.(14.18)

नान्यं गुणेभ्यः कर्तारं यदा द्रष्टानुपश्यति ।
गुणेभ्यश्च परं वेत्ति मद्भावं सोऽधिगच्छति ॥१४- १९॥

nAnya.n guNebhyaH kartAraM yadA draShTAnupashyati .
guNebhyashcha paraM vetti madbhAvaM so.adhigachchhati .. 14\-19..

na = no; anyaM = other; guNebhyaH = than the qualities; kartaaraM = performer; yadaa = when; drashhTaa = a seer; anupashyati = sees properly; guNebhyaH = to the modes of nature; cha = and; paraM = transcendental; vetti = knows; mad.hbhaavaM = to My spiritual nature; saH = he; adhigachchhati = is promoted.

When the Seer perceives no agent other than the qualities (gunas), and knows THAT which is beyond the qualities (Gunas), he enters into My nature. (14.19)

गुणानेतानतीत्य त्रीन्देही देहसमुद्भवान् ।
जन्ममृत्युजरादुःखैर्विमुक्तोऽमृतमश्नुते ॥१४- २०॥

guNAnetAnatItya trIndehI dehasamudbhavAn.h .
janmamR^ityujarAduHkhairvimukto.amR^itamashnute .. 14\-20..

guNaan.h = qualities; etaan.h = all these; atiitya = beyond; triin.h = three; dehii = the embodied; deha = the body; samudbhavaan.h = produced of;

janma = of birth; mR^ityu = death; jaraa = and old age; duHkhaiH = the distresses; vimuktaH = being freed from; amR^itaM = nectar; ashnute = he enjoys.

When the embodied goes beyond these three qualities, from which all bodies have been produced, he is liberated from birth, death, old age and sorrow, and enjoys the nectar of immortality. (14.20)

अर्जुन उवाच ।
कैर्लिङ्गैस्त्रीन्गुणानेतानतीतो भवति प्रभो ।
किमाचारः कथं चैतांस्त्रीन्गुणानतिवर्तते ॥१४- २१॥

arjuna uvAcha .
kairliN^gaistrInguNAnetAnatIto bhavati prabho .
kimAchAraH katha.n chaitA.nstrInguNAnativartate .. 14\-21..

arjuna uvaacha = Arjuna said; kaiH = by which; liN^gaiH = marks; triin.h = three; guNaan.h = qualities; etaan.h = all these; atiitaH = having transcended; bhavati = is; prabho = O my Lord; kiM = what; aachaaraH = behaviour; kathaM = how; cha = also; etaan.h = these; triin.h = three; guNaan.h = qualities; ativartate = transcends.

What are the marks of him who has crossed over the three qualities, O Lord ? How does he act and how does he go beyond these three qualities? (14.21)

श्रीभगवानुवाच ।
प्रकाशं च प्रवृत्तिं च मोहमेव च पाण्डव ।
न द्वेष्टि सम्प्रवृत्तानि न निवृत्तानि काङ्क्षति ॥१४- २२॥

shrIbhagavAnuvAcha .
prakAsha.n cha pravR^itti.n cha mohameva cha pANDava .
na dveShTi sampravR^ittAni na nivR^ittAni kAN^kShati .. 14\-22..

shriibhagavaanuvaacha = the Supreme Lord said; prakaashaM = illumination; cha = and; pravR^ittiM = attachment; cha = and; mohaM = illusion; eva cha = also; paaNDava = O son of Pandu; na dveshhTi = does not hate; ampravR^ittaani = although developed; na nivR^ittaani = nor stopping development; kaaN^kshati = desires.

The Supreme Lord said: He neither hates the presence of enlightenment, activity, and delusion nor desires for them when they are absent; and (14.22)

उदासीनवदासीनो गुणैर्यो न विचाल्यते |
गुणा वर्तन्त इत्येवं योऽवतिष्ठति नेङ्गते ||१४- २३||

udAsInavadAsIno guNairyo na vichAlyate .
guNA vartanta ityevaM yo.avatiShThati neN^gate .. 14\-23..

udaasiinavat.h = as if neutral; aasiinaH = situated; guNaiH = by the qualities; yaH = one who; na = never; vichaalyate = is agitated; guNaaH = the qualities; vartante = are acting; ityevaM = knowing thus; yaH = one who; avatishhThati = remains; na = never; iN^gate = flickers.

He seated as neutral, is not moved by the qualities (Gunas) , thinking that the Gunas (qualities) only are operating; who stands firm and does not waver; and (14.23)

समदुःखसुखः स्वस्थः समलोष्टाश्मकाञ्चनः |
तुल्यप्रियाप्रियो धीरस्तुल्यनिन्दात्मसंस्तुतिः ||१४- २४||

samaduHkhasukhaH svasthaH samaloShTAshmakA~nchanaH .
tulyapriyApriyo dhIrastulyanindAtmasa.nstutiH .. 14\-24..

sama = equal; duHkha = in distress; sukhaH = and happiness; svasthaH = being situated in himself; sama = equally; loshhTa = a lump of earth; ashma = stone; kaaJNchanaH = gold; tulya = equally disposed; priya = to the dear; apriyaH = and the undesirable; dhiiraH = steady; tulya = equal; nindaa = in defamation; aatmasa.nstutiH = and praise of himself.

- ***Balanced in pleasure and pain, self-reliant, to whom a lump of earth, a rock and gold are alike ; the same to loved and unloved, firm, the same in condemnation and in praise (14.24)***

मानापमानयोस्तुल्यस्तुल्यो मित्रारिपक्षयोः |
सर्वारम्भपरित्यागी गुणातीतः स उच्यते ||१४- २५||

mAnApamAnayostulyastulyo mitrAripakShayoH .
sarvArambhaparityAgI guNAtItaH sa uchyate .. 14\-25..

maana = in honor; apamaanayoH = and dishonour; tulyaH = equal; tulyaH = equal; mitra = of friends; ari = and enemies; pakshayoH = to the parties; sarva = of all; aarambha = endeavors; parityaagii = renouncer;

guNaatiitaH = transcendental to the material modes of nature; saH = he; uchyate = is said to be.

The one who is indifferent to honour and disgrace; who is the same to friend and foe; who has renounced the sense of doership; is said to have transcended the Gunas. (14.25)

मां च योऽव्यभिचारेण भक्तियोगेन सेवते ।
स गुणान्समतीत्यैतान्ब्रह्मभूयाय कल्पते ॥१४- २६॥

mA.n cha yo.avyabhichAreNa bhaktiyogena sevate .
sa guNAnsamatItyaitAnbrahmabhUyAya kalpate .. 14\-26..

maaM = unto Me; cha = also; yaH = a person who; avyabhichaareNa = without straying; bhaktiyogena = considering himself as part of the Supreme; sevate = renders service; saH = he; guNaan.h = the modes of material nature; samatitya = transcending; etaan.h = all these; brahmabhuyaaya = becoming seeker of the eternal ; kalpate = is fit for.

And he who servs Me exclusively by considering himself as my part, he, crossing beyond the qualities, is fit to become the seeker of the ETERNAL. (14.26)

ब्रह्मणो हि प्रतिष्ठाहममृतस्याव्ययस्य च ।
शाश्वतस्य च धर्मस्य सुखस्यैकान्तिकस्य च ॥१४- २७॥

brahmaNo hi pratiShThAhamamR^itasyAvyayasya cha .
shAshvatasya cha dharmasya sukhasyaikAntikasya cha .. 14\-27..

brahmaNaH = of the impersonal brahmajyoti; hi = certainly; pratishhThaa = the rest; ahaM = I am; amR^itasya = of the immortal; avyayasya = of the imperishable; cha = also; shaashvatasya = of the eternal; cha = and; dharmasya = of the constitutional position; sukhasya = of happiness; aikaantikasya = ultimate; cha = also

For I am the abode of the seekers of the ETERNAL, and of the indestructible nectar of immortality, of everlasting righteousness, and of unending bliss. (14.27)

ॐ तत्सदिति श्रीमद्भगवद्गीतासूपनिषत्सु
ब्रह्मविद्यायां योगशास्त्रे श्रीकृष्णार्जुनसंवादे
गुणत्रयविभागयोगो नाम चतुर्दशोऽध्यायः ॥१४॥

AUM tatsaditi shrImadbhagavadgItAsUpaniShatsu
brahmavidyAyA.n yogashAstre
shrIkR^iShNArjunasa.nvAde
guNatrayavibhAgayogo nAma chaturdasho.adhyAyaH 14

5. The Supreme Primeval Man

I am the child of Earth and starry Heaven; but my race is heavenly.

-- Orpheus

Introduction:

In the previous chapter, Lord has deliberately avoided the distinction between pure awareness and the ego created by the false perception of doership. This point of view simplifies the model of the world, consisting of the beings (Jiva) having consciousness and having a physical existence. Accordingly, the awareness of the creatures is a fraction of the Supreme Consciousness, the great Purusha. The creation is, therefore, an offspring of the union between nature (Prakriti), symbolised as primordial Female and the Supreme Consciousness (Purusha), personified as the Primaeval Man.

Chapter 15 starts with the depiction of the universe as an inverted tree, having roots upward and branches downwards, symbolising the heavenly origin. The consciousness, along with the sensory stimulation is responsible for the perception of the world seen by the creatures. The Primaeval Man is the cause of this world, and scriptures depict Him, therefore, as the heavenly root of the world tree. Seekers can cut this figurative world tree to reach the abode of the Supreme by the axe of non-attachment.

The indestructible fraction of the Supreme in a body of a being is responsible for its consciousness, proclaims bhakti-yoga. The highest entity is verily the another, the

Supreme Lord pervading all, and sustaining the three worlds.

This approach of bhakti-yoga in understanding the true nature of the Supreme also leads to the realisation that Supreme and its fraction are the same. Shankaracharya compares it with the example of an empty vas, the emptiness within which is part of the infinite space and merges into it on the destruction of the vessel.

Chapter Summary:

Lord Krishna describes the eternal Ashvattha tree having its origin in the Brahm and its branches as the cosmos visible to us. Vedic hymns are the leaves of this cosmic tree. The limbs of the cosmic tree spread everywhere, and three Gunas are its nourishment. Sense pleasures are its twigs, and its secondary roots (of ego and desires) stretch below in the human world, causing Karmic bondage. Neither its form nor its beginning, neither its end nor its existence is perceptible here on the earth.

Using the mighty axe of detachment, cutting asunder this massive tree, which represents the world, one can reach the ever peaceful, eternal abode of the Supreme Lord. Treading this path, taking refuge to that Primal Man who is the source of all creation, the seeker does not come back to this world of space-time dimension. Marching this track undeluded requires freedom from pride and delusion, conquering the attachment, with desires pacified, always aware of the Self, and liberation from the dualities of pleasure and pain.

The abode of the Supreme is the universe beyond the space-time world. That bright world does not need the sources of illumination like sun and moon. Lifeforce in the living entities is due to the fraction of the supreme Lord present in them in the form of Self. They experience the attraction towards the worldly things due to their six senses, including the mind. When an animal dies, Lord transfers all his experiences and desires of the physical world into a new body.

Using the ear, the eye, the touch, the taste and the smell, and also the mind, Lord is the real enjoyer of experiences arising from these.

Swayed by the qualities of Sattva, Rajasa and Tamasa, deluded, one does not perceive the Lord in the form of the Self who enjoys, stays and departs from the physical body. Only the knowledgable can recognise His disguised presence. The yogis striving, behold Him abiding in their heart; but the ignorant, whose intellect is not pure, do not perceive Him even though striving.

Lord is the light of all lights. The illumination coming from the sun or moon is not theirs but that of the Supreme. The vital energy of the Supreme, permeating the soil nourishes the plants, and consequently, all the beings in the world. Lord is the digestive power of all the animals. Combining with the vital breath as their life force, Lord nourishes and keeps alive the creatures.

In the form of their consciousness, Lord sits in the hearts of all beings. From Him are memory, knowledge, as well as their loss. He is the object of knowledge of all the Vedas. He as the true Self is also the author and knower of all that is knowable.

Every living entity comprises of their perishable body and imperishable, immutable Self. The Lord is declared as the supreme Self. He, the indestructible Supreme, who pervading all, sustains the three worlds, Lord is beyond the perishable body and the imperishable Self and is therefore called the Purushottama, or the Supreme Spirit.

Lord concludes this chapter by saying that He who undeluded knows Him as the Supreme spirit he, all-knowing, considers himself as His part with his whole being. Imparting this most secret teaching to Arjuna Lord says that knowing this, one becomes illuminated, and finishes his work.

Analysis:

The Cosmic Tree

Figuratively describing this world as Ashwattha tree having its roots above and branches below, Lord says that its leaves are the Vedas, and he who knows this is the knower of the Vedas.

Origin of the world is due to the power of the Supreme. The interplay of the sensual inputs and the Consciousness (Supreme residing as Self) creates this meaningful world in the minds of creatures. The potency of Supreme, the Maya (magical power) creates the illusionary world. Having its roots above points towards the divine provenance of the cosmos.

Kathopnishad (2-3-1) also says that the world is a tree having roots above. He, the Supreme is above because Brahm with Maya (illusionary power) is eternal, and is also beyond his Maya, which creates this universe. Chapter seven also explains that the Supreme as two nature, the lower one is related to the human world which we can observe and sense, and the upper one is related to the nature of the Self, which is beyond the reach of animal senses. Above and below can also be taken figuratively in that sense. What is the significance of discussing the nature of the world here? Like the tree can lead to its root similarly, the world can lead to the abode of the Supreme, its creator.

Further elaborating the nature of the world, Lord says the branches of the cosmic tree spread everywhere. The three Gunas nourish the tree; sense pleasures are its twigs. Ego and desire represent its secondary roots; stretching below in the human world, causing Karmic bondage.

Metaphorical representation of the human world existing below is because it corresponds to the lower nature of the Supreme. Ego and desire are its secondary roots extending to the human world as they are also the cause of the world created by Maya. As the three Gunas are the main constituent of nature, the cosmic tree is said to be nourished by them.

This massive cosmic tree, whose origin and end are difficult to find, can be cut by the axe of detachment. By detaching oneself from objects of desires, and going beyond the false sense of ego, one can reach the Supreme.

The Path to The Primaeval Purusha

One should seek the path, treading which there is no return. That path leads to the Primaeval Man, who is the source of all this ancient universe extended everywhere. Here again, the Self, which is the source of all creation and resides in them as their pure consciousness, is metaphorically described as the Primal Man.

Those without pride and delusion, having conquered the vice of attachment, their desires pacified, and equanimous in pleasure and pain can tread the path which leads to the dwelling of the Supreme.

The abode of the Supreme is beyond space-time dimensions formed due to interplay of consciousness and sensual inputs. The sources of light, such as the sun and moon, appear bright only due to the awareness of the living beings perceiving them. Sun, moon, fire or other luminous objects illuminate the human world. However, they do not irradiate the world of the Supreme, for he is the light of all lights himself.

The nature of Jiva (beings)

Explaining the nature of the Jiva (beings), Lord says that a portion of Himself, in the world of the creatures, becomes the Self of them and attracts the senses with mind as the sixth sense residing in the body made-up of nature.

On the explanation that Jiva is the portion of the Supreme, one may ask how can there be a portion of the Supreme who has no parts? For, if He has segments, separated in space as parts, how can he be beyond space dimension? Further, if having parts, he also becomes vulnerable to destruction on separation of them.

Bhakti yoga's interpretation of Jiva (beings) as a part of the Supreme is because it is easier to understand by a commoner. Under the influence of the ego created by Avidya (nescience), it is more natural to understand ourselves as a separate entity rather than having the

Supreme as our true Self. Avidya(ignorance) is causing the assumption of Jiva (beings) as a fraction of the Supreme and having a separate existence from Him.

Realization of the unity of Jiva and the Supreme, on the abolishment of Avidya, as one progresses on the path of Bhakti yoga, is the union of the Jiva and the God in Bhakti yoga. The Self in the body is, therefore, the Lord himself, which we perceive as a separate entity enjoying sensual pleasures under the influence of Avidya. Avidya binds the creatures (Jiva) to Parkriti (nature) due to the attraction created by sense objects through sense organs including mind and the self.

How Lord dwells in the body and departs it.

Further to clarify that the Self within is the Lord himself, the next verse (15.8) says that When the Lord abandons a body, he takes the senses to the creature which He acquires like the fragrance is transferred to another place by the blowing winds. We have already understood this transmigration from one body to another through the casual body (Karan Sharir) in chapter 13.

Enjoying the objects of the senses, using the ear, the eye, the touch sense, the taste sense and the nose, Lord presides over the minds of the creatures. When he departs or stays and enjoys, the deluded perceives that not, but the one with the eye of wisdom can only sense. In the eighth verse, Lord Krishna has unambiguously mentioned the word Ishwar (God or Lord) and says the God resides in the body of the beings and enjoys the pleasures derived from senses.

As the Lord is the Self of all creatures, he is the real subject of all sensory objects such as touch and smell. Along with the mind, sensory perceptions are felt by beings as if they are feeling it themselves.

Deluded by the magic (Maya) created by the Self, the sensory inputs and the mind, a false sense of ego is generated. Under the influence of Maya, they believe that they are the doers and enjoyers themselves. They are not aware of the presence of the God who in the form of Self in them is the enjoyer in reality, and they die when he departs. As the Self is beyond the reach of the senses, one can perceive Him only through the eyes of the wisdom. Lord further explains that the striving Yogis can notice God established in the Self. However, those who have not understood the true nature of the Self cannot behold Him.

Manifestations of God:

As explained, God is beyond the reach of our sense organs, then how one can understand His manifestations. The following section depicts the various forms of the Supreme, indicating is His omnipresence.

The light of all lights

What is the nature of the God which the Yogis understand? To explain this, Lord says the following word:

The splendour emanating from the sun, which illuminates the whole world, that radiating from the moon and the fire, that glory is from God.

Lord residing in the hearts of all beings, is the Self of all. Self is their consciousness, which construes the electro-magnetic radiations of the visible range coming from the sun, the moon or fire as a light. When light hits the retina, photoreceptors, the cells in the retina, turn the light into electrical signals. These electrical signals travel from the retina through the optic nerve to the brain, where the consciousness interprets those signals as images we see. On death, when the Self departs from the body, the same hardware, in the absence of awareness, is unable to perceive the image. The consciousness in the beings, as the manifestation of the Supreme, is, therefore, the light of all lights.

He Sustains all Life:

Permeating the earth, I support living beings by my vitality and nourish all plants, by becoming Soma, their sap. The ninth book of the Rigveda describes the Soma as an alimentative juice derived from Soma Plant. Symbolically, Lord describes himself as the nourishing sap of the plants, which sustains the beings, providing them life-giving nutrients from plants and vegetables.

God is the vital force, sustaining all lives, providing them nourishment by also nurturing the plant world.

The Digestive Fire in all Animals:

Lord further says that he becomes the digestive fire of the living organisms, and uniting with the upward and downward breath, digests the four kinds of food. Yagya metaphor describes the digestive power of the animals as the fire and the food as the offering. The oblation and libation of food to the digestive fire results in the sustenance of life.

Lord has referred to four types of foods here. The four types of food are:- the foods that are chewed, sucked, devoured or licked for consumption.

Lord is the Self of all Creatures:

Lord further says that He is sitting in the hearts of all the creatures. From Him is the memory, knowledge and loss of them. He is the object of knowledge and also the knower and author of all the Vedas.

Lord is the Self of all creatures. Describing as "sitting in their hearts" is its metaphorical narration. He is also the vital energy, which is the source of their memory, intelligence and knowledge.

Knowledge of the Self is the subject of most scriptures of spirituality, like Vedas and Vedanta. Lord as the Self is the object of knowledge of these scriptures. The authors describing these subjects in their sacred writings are only the medium performing such task, the real knowledge comes from their Self, the source of their memory and wisdom is the manifestation of the Supreme.

Supreme beyond perishable and the imperishable

Lord further says that there are two types of entities in this world, the perishable and the imperishable. Whatever we can perceive from our senses is going to vanish one day. That existing in the space-time domain is destructible. There is also one immovable, which is imperishable.

What exactly is this immortal entity? Lord has used the word "Kootasth" (कूटस्थ) for that. "Koot" is deception or illusion in Sanskrit and "Kootasth" means that which manifest itself in various forms of unreal appearances, explains Shankaracharya.

The world is nothing but the illusion created by sensory perceptions and the Self. This power of the Supreme to create an illusion is Maya (magic)which is a technical term used to describe the unreal existence of the world in Indian philosophy. According to Sankaracharya, Maya creates illusions and deceptions projecting the perishable world but is imperishable itself.

You may like to note, however, that it is the animal consciousness which creates the illusionary world using sensory signals. If the world is Maya or illusion, then the Self, in the form of animal consciousness is its creator which resides unmoved in it and is therefore rightly mentioned as imperishable "Kootasth".

Furthermore, "Kootasth" can also be the perceived sense of the Self of a bhakti-yogi which is different from the Supreme Self as understood by a Gyan-Yogi. It is the consciousness of the beings which they believe to be themselves. Until their Self merges and becomes one with the Supreme, Bhakti-Yogi considers it as a part of the Supreme. As a part of the Supreme for a Bhakti-Yogi, Self, though distinct from the Supreme, is imperishable. Lord might have referred "self of the beings" as "Kootasth" because their consciousness, along with sensory inputs creates the illusion(Maya).

Another explanation of the imperishable is the energy-mass system. The objects of the perceivable world may be transient, but, the energy-mass system, forming them is indestructible. In other words, during the process of abolition of an object, only the form is changed, whereas, mass-energy in the process remains conserved. Lord might have described mass-energy as the "Kootasth" as it is the common factor in various deceptive forms of the objects, which is imperishable.

Considering the interpretation in verse 19 later on, which talks about viewing oneself as part of the Supreme with one's whole being, the explanation of the Bhakti-yoga for "Kootasth" as the Self of the individuals appears more appropriate.

Distinct from these two, the perishable and imperishable -and untainted by the evils of them, eternal, real, intelligent and free by nature is the Supreme. Declared as the Highest Spirit, He is quite different from the two entities which we have described above. He is the eternal, omniscient Lord who permeates the three worlds-- Bhuh (earth, or the objects which exis, or the manifested nature), Bhuvah (space, unmanifested nature), and Swah(the Self or the consciousness), and sustains them by his mere existence.

Now, let us examine the concept of three worlds, which is found quite often in Indian scriptures. Bhuh is a Sanskrit root which means - to exist. "Bhuh" may refer to the earth as it is the source of all that exists. It also means all animate and inanimate objects. "Bhuh", therefore, is all that is part of our world, which we can see, touch and feel with our senses.

The second world is "Bhuvah", which is the space in Sanskrit. It is the emptiness that acts as a container for things to exist and also the interstellar territory containing nothing. Further, it is also the space between subatomic particles such as electrons and protons or nucleus.

The third is "Swah" which means the Self in Sanskrit. Swah is the consciousness of the creatures. It is the subjects of all experiences and feelings, and also the source of memory, intelligence, and knowledge. For a Gyan-Yogi, it is the common element pervading all, the eternal, omniscience and formless Supreme itself. Everblissful in its purest form, it is not tainted by the passionate acts of the individuals and is also called as heaven. The "Bhuh" and "Bhuvah" worlds are the creation of the "Svah" which are accessible to individuals. The world of Swah, having its existence beyond the space and time, is not reachable by animal senses. "Bhuvah" or space though part of the human world, is accessible to our us generally through enhancing devices like microscopes and telescopes.

Pervading all the three worlds, that is the objects that exist, the emptiness, and also the consciousness of the individuals, the Supreme Lord is the cause and sustainer of them.

Gayatri Mantra, composed by Maharshi Vishwamitra, from 3rd book of Rigveda echoes a similar concept. The famous mantra is as follows:

ॐ भूर्भुवः स्वः।
तत्सवितुर्वरेण्यं भर्गो देवस्य धीमहि ।
धियो यो नः प्रचोदयात् ॥RV 3,62.10॥

in ITRANS

OM bhUrbhuvaH svaH . tatsaviturvareNyaM bhargo devasya dhImahi . dhiyo yo naH prachodayAt.

The formless eternal conscious and blissful supreme Lord represented symbolically by OM, which is manifested as the things which exist (bhooH)and can be seen or observed, the emptiness (bhuvaH) in which the things exist and also as the eternal consciousness (svaH) which is the real subject of all observations in all beings (means which sees when you see, which hears when you hear etc.) that (tat) cause of the existence of all the universe, the glorious one (Savitr) has manifested in the form of brightness in the pre-dawn sky (Savitri), we pray to that most excellent, glorious, supreme bliss (vareNyam). That is the real brightness of the shining ones (bhrgodevasya"), that is the light of lights through which we see the brightness of the rising sun, and is the supreme intellect (dhimahi). May That (yaH) guide our (naH) intellect (dhiyaH) and propel it forward (prachodayAt).

The mantra finds significant importance in Vedic and Vedanta literature as well as in Buddhism. The prayer is secular and as can be understood from the meaning explained can be recited by a person following any religious belief. The last few verses of this chapter also reiterate a similar concept.

The Purushottama, the Highest Spirit is a popular name of the Lord, the etymology of which has been described here by the Lord himself, to elaborate His unsurpassed sovereignty.

Proclaiming that He transcends the perishable, illusionary world described as the Ashwatha tree, and also the imperishable that constitutes the seed of that tree, Lord elaborated his unequalled supremacy to enlighten us about his true nature in the form of the Self of all creatures. The world and the Vedas, therefore, declare Him as the Highest Spirit.

The undeluded, who knows the Lord as the Supreme Spirit, comprehending all, he considers himself with his whole being as a part of the Supreme Lord. Underscoring the importance of the knowledge explained above, Lord praises it by saying that this is the most secret teaching, knowing which one becomes illuminated and nothing is left to be finished in this world by such a person.

Original Sanskrit with Word Meanings, Transliteration and Translation (Chapter-15)

अथ पञ्चदशोऽध्यायः । पुरुषोत्तमयोगः

atha pa~nchadasho.adhyAyaH . puruShottamayogaH

Here begins the fifteenth chapter (puruShottamayogaH)

श्रीभगवानुवाच ।
ऊर्ध्वमूलमधःशाखमश्वत्थं प्राहुरव्ययम् ।
छन्दांसि यस्य पर्णानि यस्तं वेद स वेदवित् ॥१५- १॥

shrIbhagavAnuvAcha .
UrdhvamUlamadhaHshAkhamashvatthaM prAhuravyayam.h .
chhandA.nsi yasya parNAni yasta.n veda sa vedavit.h .. 15\-1..

shriibhagavaanuvaacha = the Supreme Lord said; uurdhvamuulaM = with roots above; adhaH = downwards; shaakhaM = branches; ashvatthaM = a banyan tree; praahuH = is said; avyayaM = eternal; chhandaa.nsi = the Vedic hymns; yasya = of which; parNaani = the leaves; yaH = anyone who; taM = that; veda = knows; saH = he; vedavit.h = the knower of the Vedas.

The Supreme Lord said: They speak of the eternal Ashvattha tree having its origin above (in unmanifest Brahman) and its branches below (in the cosmos) whose leaves are the (Vedic) hymns. One who understands this is a knower of the Vedas. (15.01)

अधश्चोर्ध्वं प्रसृतास्तस्य शाखा
गुणप्रवृद्धा विषयप्रवालाः ।
अधश्च मूलान्यनुसन्ततानि
कर्मानुबन्धीनि मनुष्यलोके ॥१५- २॥

adhashchordhvaM prasR^itAstasya shAkhA
guNapravR^iddhA viShayapravAlAH .
adhashcha mUlAnyanusantatAni
karmAnubandhIni manuShyaloke .. 15\-2..

adhaH = downward; cha = and; uurdhvaM = upward; prasR^itaaH = extended; tasya = its; shaakhaaH = branches; guNa = by the qualities; pravR^iddhaaH = developed; vishhaya = sense objects; pravaalaaH = twigs, buds; adhaH = downward; cha = and; muulaani = roots; anusantataani = extended; karma = to work; anubandhiini = bound; manushhyaloke = in the world of human society.

The branches (of the cosmic tree) spread below and above (everywhere). The tree is nourished by the Gunas; sense pleasures are its twigs; and its roots (of ego and desires) stretch below in the human world causing Karmic bondage. (15.02)

न रूपमस्येह तथोपलभ्यते
नान्तो न चादिर्न च सम्प्रतिष्ठा।
अश्वत्थमेनं सुविरूढमूलं
असङ्गशस्त्रेण दृढेन छित्त्वा ॥१५- ३॥

na rUpamasyeha tathopalabhyate
nAnto na chAdirna cha sampratiShThA .
ashvatthamenaM suvirUDhamUlaM
asaN^gashastreNa dR^iDhena chhittvA .. 15\-3..

na = not; ruupaM = the form; asya = of this tree; iha = in this world; tathaa = also; upalabhyate = can be perceived; na = never; antaH = end; na = never; cha = also; aadiH = beginning; na = never; cha = also; sampratishhThaa = the foundation; ashvatthaM = banyan tree; enaM = this; suviruuDha = strongly; muulaM = rooted; asaN^gashastreNa = by the weapon of detachment; dR^iDhena = strong; chhittva = cutting.

Neither its form nor its beginning, neither its end nor its existence is perceptible here on the earth. Having cut these firm roots of the Ashvattha tree by the mighty axe of detachment. (15.03)

ततः पदं तत्परिमार्गितव्यं
यस्मिन्गता न निवर्तन्ति भूयः।
तमेव चाद्यं पुरुषं प्रपद्ये।
यतः प्रवृत्तिः प्रसृता पुराणी ॥१५- ४॥

tataH padaM tatparimArgitavyaM

yasmingatA na nivartanti bhUyaH .
tameva chAdyaM puruShaM prapadye .
yataH pravR^ittiH prasR^itA purANI .. 15\-4..

tataH = thereafter; padaM = situation; tat.h = that; parimaargitavyaM = has to be searched out; yasmin.h = where; gataaH = going; na = never; nivartanti = they come back; bhuuyaH = again; taM = to Him; eva = certainly; cha = also; aadyaM = original; purushhaM = Purush, the brahma; prapadye = surrender; yataH = from whom; pravR^ittiH = the beginning; prasR^itaa = extended; puraaNii = very old.

That path beyond may be sought, treading which there is no return. I take refuge to that Primal Man from where the ancient manifestation comes forth 15.04

निर्मानमोहा जितसङ्गदोषा
अध्यात्मनित्या विनिवृत्तकामाः ।
द्वन्द्वैर्विमुक्ताः सुखदुःखसंज्ञैर्-
गच्छन्त्यमूढाः पदमव्ययं तत् ॥१५- ५॥
nirmAnamohA jitasaN^gadoShA
adhyAtmanityA vinivR^ittakAmAH .
dvandvairvimuktAH sukhaduHkhasa.nGYair\-
gachchhantyamUDhAH padamavyayaM tat.h .. 15\-5..

niH = without; maana = false prestige; mohaH = and illusion; jita = having conquered; saN^ga = of association; doshhaaH = the faults; adhyaatma = in knowledge of self; nityaaH = in eternity; vinivR^itta = disassociated; kaamaaH = from lust; dvandvaiH = from the dualities; vimuktaH = liberated; sukhaduHkha = happiness and distress; sa.nGYaiH = named; gachchhanti = attain; amuuDhaaH = unbewildered; padaM = to the goal; avyayaM = eternal; tat.h = that.

Those who are free from pride and delusion, who have conquered the evil of attachment, who are constantly dwelling in the Self, with desires pacified, who are free from the dualities known as pleasure and pain; they tread, undeluded, that indestructible path. (15.05)

न तद्भासयते सूर्यो न शशाङ्को न पावकः ।

यद्गत्वा न निवर्तन्ते तद्धाम परमं मम ||१५- ६||

na tadbhAsayate sUryo na shashAN^ko na pAvakaH .
yadgatvA na nivartante taddhAma paramaM mama .. 15\-6..

na = not; tat.h = that; bhaasayate = illuminates; suuryaH = the sun; na = nor; shashaaN^kaH = the moon; na = nor; paavakaH = fire, electricity; yat.h = where; gatvaa = going; na = never; nivartante = they come back; tad.hdhaama = that abode; paramaM = supreme; mama = My.

The sun does not illumine there, nor the moon, nor the fire. That is My supreme abode. Having reached there they do not come back.(15.06)

mamaivA.nsho jIvaloke jIvabhUtaH sanAtanaH .
manaHShaShThAnIndriyANi prakR^itisthAni karShati .. 15\-7..

ममैवांशो जीवलोके जीवभूतः सनातनः |
मनःषष्ठानीन्द्रियाणि प्रकृतिस्थानि कर्षति ||१५- ७||

mama = My; eva = certainly; a.nshaH = fragmental particle; jiivaloke = in the world; jiivabhuutaH = living entity; sanaatanaH = eternal; manaH = with the mind; shhashhThaaNi = the six; indriyaaNi = senses; prakR^iti = in material nature; sthaani = situated; karshhati = is struggling hard.

Living entities are My eternal indivisible fragment indeed, they get bound due to the attraction of six sensory faculties, including the mind. (15.07)

शरीरं यदवाप्नोति यच्चाप्युत्क्रामतीश्वरः |
गृहीत्वैतानि संयाति वायुर्गन्धानिवाशयात् ||१५- ८||

sharIra.n yadavApnoti yachchApyutkrAmatIshvaraH .
gR^ihItvaitAni sa.nyAti vAyurgandhAnivAshayAt.h .. 15\-8.

shariiraM = the body; yat.h = as; avaapnoti = gets; yat.h = as; chaapi = also; utkraamati = gives up; iishvaraH = the lord, God; gR^ihiitvaa = taking; etaani = all these; sa.nyaati = goes away; vaayuH = the air; gandhaan.h = smells; iva = like; ashayaat.h = from their source.

When the Lord acquires a body and when He abandons it, He seizes these and goes with them, as the wind takes fragrances from their seats. ((15.08)

श्रोत्रं चक्षुः स्पर्शनं च रसनं घ्राणमेव च ।

अधिष्ठाय मनश्चायं विषयानुपसेवते ॥१५- ९॥

shrotra.n chakShuH sparshana.n cha rasanaM ghrANameva cha .

adhiShThAya manashchAyaM viShayAnupasevate .. 15\-9..

shrotraM = ears; chakshuH = eyes; sparshanaM = touch; cha = also; rasanaM = tongue; ghraaNaM = smelling power; eva = also; cha = and; adhishhThaaya = being situated in; manaH = mind; cha = also; ayaM = he; vishhayaan.h = sense objects; upasevate = enjoys.

Using the ear, the eye, the touch, the taste and the smell, and also the mind, He enjoys the objects of the senses.(15.09)

उत्क्रामन्तं स्थितं वापि भुञ्जानं वा गुणान्वितम् ।

विमूढा नानुपश्यन्ति पश्यन्ति ज्ञानचक्षुषः ॥१५- १०॥

utkrAmantaM sthitaM vApi bhu~njAnaM vA guNAnvitam.h .

vimUDhA nAnupashyanti pashyanti GYAnachakShuShaH .. 15\-10..

utkraamantaM = quitting the body; sthitaM = situated in the body; vaapi = either; bhuJNjaanaM = enjoying; vaa = or; guNaanvitaM = under the spell of the modes of material nature; vimuuDhaaH = foolish persons; na = never; anupashyanti = can see; pashyanti = can see; GYaanachakshushhaH = those who have the eyes of knowledge.

When He departs, stays, or enjoys, swayed by the qualities; the deluded perceive not; they see, who possess the eye of knowledge. (15.10)

यतन्तो योगिनश्चैनं पश्यन्त्यात्मन्यवस्थितम् ।

यतन्तोऽप्यकृतात्मानो नैनं पश्यन्त्यचेतसः ॥१५- ११॥

yatanto yoginashchainaM pashyantyAtmanyavasthitam.h .
yatanto.apyakR^itAtmAno nainaM pashyantyachetasaH .. 15\-11..

yatantaH = endeavouring, striving; yoginaH = Yogis; cha = also; enaM = this; pashyanti = can see; aatmani = in the self; avasthitaM

= situated; yatantaH = endeavouring, striving; api = although; akR^itaatmaanaH = those without self-realization; na = do not; enaM = this; pashyanti = see; achetasaH = not so conscious.

The yogis striving behold Him abiding in their self; but the ignorant, whose intellect is not pure, do not perceive Him even though striving. (15.11)

यदादित्यगतं तेजो जगद्भासयतेऽखिलम् ।
यच्चन्द्रमसि यच्चाग्नौ तत्तेजो विद्धि मामकम् ॥१५- १२॥

yadAdityagataM tejo jagadbhAsayate.akhilam.h .
yachchandramasi yachchAgnau tattejo viddhi mAmakam.h .. 15\-12.

yat.h = that which; aadityagataM = in the sunshine; tejaH = splendour; jagat.h = the whole world; bhaasayate = illuminates; akhilaM = entirely; yat.h = that which; chandramasi = in the moon; yat.h = that which; cha = also; agnau = in fire; tat.h = that; tejaH = splendour; viddhi = understand; maamakaM = from Me.

The light that coming from the sun illumines the whole world; and which is in the moon, and in the fire; know that light to be Mine. (15.12)

गामाविश्य च भूतानि धारयाम्यहमोजसा ।
पुष्णामि चौषधीः सर्वाः सोमो भूत्वा रसात्मकः ॥१५- १३॥

gAmAvishya cha bhUtAni dhArayAmyahamojasA .
puShNAmi chauShadhIH sarvAH somo bhUtvA rasAtmakaH .. 15\-13.

gaaM = the planets, the earth; aavishya = entering; cha = also; bhuutaanii = the living entities; dhaarayaami = sustain; ahaM = I; ojasaa = by My energy; pushhNaami = am nourishing; cha = and; aushhadhiiH = vegetables; sarvaaH = all; somaH = the moon; bhuutvaa = becoming; rasaatmakaH = supplying the juice.

Permeating the Earth, I support beings by My vital energy, and having become the delicious Soma, I nourish all plants. (15.13)

अहं वैश्वानरो भूत्वा प्राणिनां देहमाश्रितः ।
प्राणापानसमायुक्तः पचाम्यन्नं चतुर्विधम् ॥१५- १४॥

aha.n vaishvAnaro bhUtvA prANinA.n dehamAshritaH .
prANApAnasamAyuktaH pachAmyanna.n chaturvidham.h .. 15\-14..

ahaM = I; vaishvaanaraH = the digesting fire; bhuutvaa = becoming; praaNinaaM = of all living entities; dehaM = in the bodies; aashritaH = situated; praaNa = the outgoing air; apaana = the down-going air; samaayuktaH = keeping in balance; pachaami = I digest; annaM = foodstuff; chaturvidhaM = the four kinds.

Becoming the digestive fire, I remain in the body of all living beings; uniting with vital breaths, the Prana and Apana, I digest all four kinds of food; and (15.14)

सर्वस्य चाहं हृदि सन्निविष्टो
मत्तः स्मृतिर्ज्ञानमपोहनञ्च ।
वेदैश्च सर्वैरहमेव वेद्यो
वेदान्तकृद्वेदविदेव चाहम् ॥१५- १५॥

sarvasya chAhaM hR^idi sanniviShTo
mattaH smR^itirGYAnamapohana~ncha .
vedaishcha sarvairahameva vedyo
vedAntakR^idvedavideva chAham.h .. 15\-15..

sarvasya = of all living beings; cha = and; ahaM = I; hR^idi = in the heart; sannivishhTaH = situated; mattaH = from Me; smR^itiH = remembrance; GYaanaM = knowledge; apohanaM = forgetfulness; cha = and; vedaiH = by the Vedas; cha = also; sarvaiH = all; ahaM = I am; eva = certainly; vedyaH = knowable; vedaantakR^it.h = the compiler of the Vedanta; vedavit.h = the knower of the Vedas; eva = certainly; cha = and; ahaM = I.

And I am seated in the hearts of all: from Me are memory, knowledge, as well as their loss ;
I am the object of knowledge of all the Vedas, I am indeed the author of the Vedanta as well as the knower of the Vedas.15.15

द्वाविमौ पुरुषौ लोके क्षरश्चाक्षर एव च ।
क्षरः सर्वाणि भूतानि कूटस्थोऽक्षर उच्यते ॥१५- १६॥

dvAvimau puruShau loke kSharashchAkShara eva cha .
kSharaH sarvANi bhUtAni kUTastho.akShara uchyate .. 15\-16..

dvau = two; imau = these; purushhau = living entities; loke = in the world; ksharaH = fallible; cha = and; aksharaH = infallible; eva =

certainly; cha = and; sharaH = fallible; sarvaaNi = all; bhuutaanii = living entities; kuuTasthaH = in the Maya, immutable; aksharaH = infallible; uchyate = is said.

There are these two entities in the world, the perishable and the imperishable : the perishable comprises all creatures, the immutable is called the imperishable. (15.16)

उत्तमः पुरुषस्त्वन्यः परमात्मेत्युधाहृतः |
यो लोकत्रयमाविश्य बिभर्त्यव्यय ईश्वरः ||१५- १७||

uttamaH puruShastvanyaH paramAtmetyudhAhR^itaH .
yo lokatrayamAvishya bibhartyavyaya IshvaraH .. 15\-17..

uttamaH = the best; purushhaH = personality; tu = but; anyaH = another; parama = the supreme; aatmaa = self; iti = thus; udaahR^itaH = is said; yaH = who; loka = of the universe; trayaM = the three divisions; aavishya = entering; bibharti = is maintaining; avyayaH = inexhaustible; iishvaraH = the Lord, the Supeme.

The highest entity is verily the another, declared as the supreme SELF, He, who pervading all, sustains the three worlds, the indestructible Supreme.(15.17)

यस्मात्क्षरमतीतोऽहमक्षरादपि चोत्तमः |
अतोऽस्मि लोके वेदे च प्रथितः पुरुषोत्तमः ||१५- १८||

yasmAtkSharamatIto.ahamakSharAdapi chottamaH .
ato.asmi loke vede cha prathitaH puruShottamaH .. 15\-18.

yasmaat.h = because; ksharaM = destructible; atiitaH = beyond; ahaM = I am; aksharaat.h = imperishable; api = also; cha = and; uttamaH = the best; ataH = therefore; asmi = I am; loke = in the world; vede = in the Vedic literature; cha = and; prathitaH = celebrated; purushhottamaH = as the Supreme Purush or Spirit.

I am beyond the perishable body, and higher than the imperishable ; therefore, I am known in this world and in the Vedas as Purushottama, or the Supreme Spirit. (15.18)

यो मामेवमसम्मूढो जानाति पुरुषोत्तमम् |
स सर्वविद्भजति मां सर्वभावेन भारत ||१५- १९||

yo mAmevamasammUDho jAnAti puruShottamam.h .
sa sarvavidbhajati mAM sarvabhAvena bhArata .. 15\-19.

yaH = anyone who; maaM = Me; evaM = thus; asammuuDhaH = without a doubt; jaanaati = knows; purushhottamaM = the Supreme

Spirit, Supreme Purusha; saH = he; sarvavit.h = the knower of everything; bhajati = considers himself part ; maaM = unto Me; sarvabhaavena = in all respects; bhaarata = O son of Bharata.

He who undeluded knows Me thus as the Supreme spirit he, all-knowing, considers himself as part of Me with his whole being, O Bharata. (15.19)

इति गुह्यतमं शास्त्रमिदमुक्तं मयानघ |
एतद्बुद्ध्वा बुद्धिमान्स्यात्कृतकृत्यश्च भारत ||१५- २०||
iti guhyatamaM shAstramidamuktaM mayAnagha .
etadbud.hdhvA buddhimAnsyAtkR^itakR^ityashcha bhArata .. 15\-20..

iti = thus; guhyatamaM = the most confidential; shaastraM = revealed scripture; idaM = this; uktaM = disclosed; mayaa = by Me; anagha = O sinless one; etat.h = this; bud.hdhvaa = understanding; buddhimaan.h = intelligent; syaat.h = one becomes; kR^itakR^ityaH = the most perfect in his endeavors; cha = and; bhaarata = O son of Bharata.

Thus by Me this most secret teaching has been told, O sinless one. This known, one becomes illuminated, and finishes his work, O Bharata. (15.20)

ॐ तत्सदिति श्रीमद्भगवद्गीतासूपनिषत्सु
ब्रह्मविद्यायां योगशास्त्रे श्रीकृष्णार्जुन संवादे
पुरुषोत्तमयोगो नाम पञ्चदशोऽध्यायः ||१५||

AUM tatsaditi shrImadbhagavadgItAsUpaniShatsu
brahmavidyAyA.n yogashAstre shrIkR^iShNArjuna sa.nvAde
puruShottamayogo nAma pa~nchadasho.adhyAyaH .. 15..

16. The Divine and the Demonic Mind

देवासुरा ह वै यत्र संयेतिरे उभये प्राजापत्यास्तद्ध देवा उद्गीथमाजहुरनेनैनानभिभविष्याम इति ॥ Chandogya १२.१ ॥.

(The Divine and the Demons are both the progeny of the Prajapati, yet they fought among themselves. The Divine then adopted the path of Udgitha, thinking they would thereby be able to overcome the demons. ----- Chandoya Upnishad 1.2.1)

Introduction:

The chapter uses various popular symbolisms such as Deva, Ausra, Swarg and Narak etc. "Deva" a Sanskrit word, is derived from root "div", which means "to shine". Deva, in this chapter, are the people with glorious attributes, Asura, on the other hand, are the people with disgraceful characteristics. The nearest equivalent of "Deva" in English is Divine and of Asura is Demon. "Sura" is another name for Devas and, therefore, Asura is the opposite of Deva.

Variety of people we come across during our interactions, some are splendidly excellent, while the others are viciously evil, yet they are our fellow human beings. As the Chandongya Upanishad says, Devas and Asuras are both the progeny of Prajapati.

Divine qualities lead to sustenance and bliss, whereas the demonic one leads to destruction and grief. Another set of leading metaphor, "Swarg" and "Narak", is widely used in Vedantic and subsequent literature. "Swah" is

Self in Sanskrit and "ga" is abiding in. "Swarg" is therefore abiding in the Self, indicating towards an inner world, the world of the Supreme Self, which is ever blissful. Swarga, an imaginary blissful place, is translated loosely as heaven by most western scholars.

"Narak", on the other hand, is derived from "Nara", which means men and a nominal common suffix "ka". "Naraka" is, therefore, the world of men, as opposed to the world of the Self, and is full of desire, disease, despair and distress.

How the demonic and divine qualities can affect internal peace, harmony, and bliss, and how they influence the progression of an in individual to the path of freedom from agony is the subject of discussion of this discourse.

Chapter Summary:

Lord Krishna starts the discourse elaborating the quality of a person having divine attributes. Enumerating such qualities as Fearlessness, purity of heart, perseverance in the yoga of knowledge, charity, sense restraint, sacrifice, the study of the scriptures, austerity, straightforwardness, are the divine virtues of a person, says Lord Krishna.

Further, Lord says, that such a person also have nonviolence, truthfulness, absence of anger, renunciation, equanimity, abstaining from the malicious talk, compassion for all creatures, freedom from greed, gentleness, modesty, steadiness as his essential qualities.

Furthermore, splendour, forgiveness, fortitude, cleanliness, absence of hatred, and absence of pride; these are the qualities of those endowed with divine virtues, says Lord Krishna. Contrarily, hypocrisy, arrogance, pride, anger, harshness, and ignorance; these are the marks of those who are born with demonic qualities.

After describing the qualities of the person with divine properties in length, Lord proceeds to elaborate in detail the attributes of those having demonic traits. Such people say that the world is without truth, without a substratum, without a God, brought about by mutual union and caused by lust (or Kaama) alone and nothing else. Adhering to this view, having lost themselves, such individuals with small intellect and cruel deeds, are born as enemies for the destruction of the world.

Filled with insatiable desires, hypocrisy, pride, and arrogance; holding wrong views due to delusion; they act with impure motives. Obsessed with great anxiety until death, considering sense gratification as their highest aim, convinced that it is everything; bound by hundreds of ties of desire and enslaved by lust and anger; they strive to obtain wealth by unlawful means for the fulfilment of desires.

Thinking about achievements, and fulfilling desires in the future, acquiring wealth and planning to obtain more in the future; winning over enemies and intending to win more; they believe that they are the Lord, they are the successful, the enjoyers, all-powerful and happy. Considering themselves as rich, born in a noble family, and the greatest, they plan for charity and sacrifice with an intent to rejoice; thus deluded by ignorance, and bewildered by many fancies; entangled in the net of delusion; addicted to the enjoyment of sensual pleasures; they fall into agony. Self-conceited, stubborn, filled with pride and intoxication of wealth; they perform Yajna only in name, for a show, and not according to scriptural injunction. Clinging to egoism, power, arrogance, lust, and anger; these malicious people hate the Lord (who dwells as their Self) in their own body and the bodies of the others. These haters, cruel, sinful, and mean people of the world, take birth with demonic qualities again and again and these deluded ones suffer from severe distress without ever attaining the blissful abode of the Supreme Self.

Lust, anger, and greed are the three gates of suffering, and one must learn to control them to avoid distress. To attain perfection, happiness and the supreme Goal, one must liberate from these three gates of hell. Therefore, let the scripture be your authority in determining what should be done and what should not be done. You should perform your duty following the scriptural injunction, says Lord Krishna.

Analysis:

People have Divine and Demonic Qualities

The sixteenth discourse of Bhagavad Gita uses a well-known Vedic symbolism -- Deva and Ausra. "Deva" a Sanskrit word, is derived from root "div", which means "to shine". Deva, described in this chapter, are the people with glorious attributes, Asura, on the other hand, are the people with disgraceful characteristics. The nearest equivalent of "Deva" in English is Divine and of Asura is Demon. We come across various people during our interactions, some are splendidly excellent, while the others are viciously evil, yet they are our fellow human beings. As the Chandongya Upanishad says, Devas and Asuras are both the progeny of Prajapati. Of these two, traits of Devas lead to liberation, and those of Asuras lead to bondage and destruction.

Divine qualities lead to liberation:

Accordingly, Lord Krishna describes the attributes of Devas to advise its acceptance and that of Asuras to suggest its rejection. First three verses in this chapter describe the qualities of Devas. Describing the nature of Devas, Lord Krishna says- fearlessness, purity of heart, steadfastness in the yoga of knowledge, almsgiving, self-restraint, selfless service, self-study, constant efforts, and uprightness are the characteristics of people having nature of devas.

Nonviolence, truthfulness, absence of anger, renunciation, equanimity, abstaining from a malicious talk, compassion for all creatures, freedom from greed, gentleness, modesty, absence of fickleness are the traits of a divine person. Splendour, forgiveness, fortitude, cleanliness, absence of malice, and absence of pride; these are the qualities of those endowed with divine virtues.

Describing the qualities of a divine person, the first quality Lord lists out is fearlessness. Understanding the true nature of the Self and the Supreme erases perceived threats, and eliminates scarcity mentality. Steadfastness in the yoga of knowledge is the foundation of fearlessness, and is an essential trait of a divine person. Instead of confronting others, such people try to build a collaborative relationship by building common grounds.

They extend trust to others and look for win-win solutions.

Just as practising hostility escalates violence, practising kindness and compassion escalates peace. Nonviolence, truthfulness, absence of anger, renunciation, equanimity, compassion for all creatures, freedom from greed, gentleness, and modesty, all emanate from the true understanding of the Self.

The glory and fearlessness come from fearless righteous conduct and non-attachment. These attributes emanate from the foundation of the realization of the true Self. This thought imparts mental strength. The understanding that one is not merely a physical body, not the psychological self, but the eternal, omnipotent and omnipresent conscious witness enables one to become prideless.

Demonic qualities lead to bondage

Worry, anxiety, and fear stem from your thoughts about a thing, person or an idea one has an attachment with. It may be due to the insecurity arising out of losing something, someone or someone's attention. The nescience creates an attachment to objects, people or ideas, which is the root cause of these emotions.

Further, describing the marks of a person having demonic qualities, Lord says, they exhibit hypocrisy, arrogance, pride, anger, harshness, and ignorance. One can understand that the root cause of such qualities is the absence of true knowledge about the Self.

Consequences of Demonic qualities

Lord further says that there are two kinds of people in this world, the divine and the demonic, and he then proceeds to explain about the persons having demonic qualities.

People with wicked qualities are bewildered in most situations about their actions. The lack of understanding of their true nature of existence results in deceitfulness, impure objectives, and conduct resulting in little or no fulfilment.

The Carnal world view:

They perceive the world without ultimate reality and believe that the world exists of its own, without the Supreme. They think that the mutual union under the influence of lust is the cause of the world. Except lust there is no other cause of the universe. According to such people, believing that they are thinking rationally, they consider sexual passion as the sole cause of all living creatures.

Guided by their false belief, they lose touch with their true self and act to fulfil their insatiable desires and may engage in cruel deeds destroying the world. People with evil qualities having unquenchable cravings, hypocrisy, pride and arrogance, caused by wrong views due to delusion, act with impure motives resulting in great anxiety until death.

Their actions are guided by their several desires, lust and anger and they don't even hesitate to fulfil them at the cost of others. They easily indulge in unsustainable practices to accumulate wealth to fulfil their wants and do not hesitate even to adopt illegal means to acquire money.

Demonic people are enemies of the self and the world

Filled with pride and intoxication of wealth they even perform charity to satisfy their ego. Their actions are for showing off to the world, not for their satisfaction. Such actions, under the influence of egoism, power, arrogance, lust and anger are against the Supreme enshrined in the bodies of themselves and the others. Their actions are unsustainable and against the people whom they perceive insignificant. Such actions even create internal conflicts in their minds and create an agitated state.

As the desires are ever insatiable, the unquenchable thirst to satisfy them unsettles their minds and even after death, they return to this world hoping to fulfil their unappeasable desires binding them in a bond of karma.

The intention is more important than the act itself:

In verse 16.15 and 16.16, Lord has clarified that

आढ्योऽभिजनवानस्मि कोऽन्योऽस्ति सद्दशो मया |
यक्ष्ये दास्यामि मोदिष्य इत्यज्ञानविमोहिताः ||१६- १५||

One thinking himself as born in a superior family, thinking himself as the greatest, even giving alms and performing sacrifice is deluded by ignorance. Such deluded persons fall into deep dark hell.

Hell here is a figurative world conveying the meaning that such persons suffer from great distress, mental agony and frustration. Hell is not any real place but depicts the mental condition of a person.

The Three Gates of the Hell:

As described before, "Swah" is Self in Sanskrit and "ga" is abiding in. "Swarg" is therefore abiding in the Self, indicating towards an inner world, the world of the Supreme Self, which is ever blissful. Swarga, an imaginary blissful place, is translated loosely as heaven by most western scholars.

"Narak", on the other hand, is derived from "Nara", which means men and a nominal common suffix "ka". "Naraka" is, therefore, the world of men, as opposed to the world of the Self, and is full of desire, disease, despair and distress. It is loosely translated as hell by western scholars. "Naraka" implies a state leading to immense sufferings, distress and mental agony.

Actions governed by lust, anger and greed lead to enormous distress and therefore they are collectively referred to as the three gates of "Naraka" or hell.

Lord advises that the one who overcomes lust, anger and greed does the best and attains the supreme goal. On the other hand, the one acting under the influence of desires neither attains perfection, nor happiness. He doesn't reach the supreme goal. The scriptures define in detail the acts, intentions and methods that propagate harmony, composure and serenity. One is advised therefore to follow the scriptures to understand what should be done and what should not be done.

Original Sanskrit with Word Meanings, Transliteration and Translation (Chapter-16)

अथ षोडशोऽध्यायः । दैवासुरसम्पद्विभागयोगः

atha ShoDasho.adhyAyaH .
daivAsurasampadvibhAgayogaH
Here begins the sixteenth chapter
(daivAsurasampadvibhAgayogaH

श्रीभगवानुवाच ।
अभयं सत्त्वसंशुद्धिर्ज्ञानयोगव्यवस्थितिः ।
दानं दमश्च यज्ञश्च स्वाध्यायस्तप आर्जवम् ॥१६- १॥

shrIbhagavAnuvAcha .
abhayaM sattvasa.nshuddhirGYAnayogavyavasthitiH .
dAnaM damashcha yaGYashcha svAdhyAyastapa Arjavam.h .. 16\-1..

shriibhagavaanuvaacha = the Supreme Lord said; abhayaM = fearlessness; sattvasa.nshuddhiH = purification of one's existence;GYaana = in knowledge; yoga = of linking up; vyavasthitiH = the situation; daanaM = charity; damaH = controlling the mind; cha = and; yaGYaH = performance of sacrifice; cha = and; svaadhyaayaH = study of Vedic literature; tapaH = austerity; aarjavaM = simplicity.

The Supreme Lord said: Fearlessness, purity of heart, perseverance in the yoga of knowledge, charity, sense restraint, sacrifice, study of the scriptures, austerity, and straightforwardness; (16.01)

अहिंसा सत्यमक्रोधस्त्यागः शान्तिरपैशुनम् ।
दया भूतेष्वलोलुप्त्वं मार्दवं ह्रीरचापलम् ॥१६- २॥

ahi.nsA satyamakrodhastyAgaH shAntirapaishunam.h .
dayA bhUteShvaloluptvaM mArdavaM hrIrachApalam.h .. 16\-2..

ahi.nsaa = nonviolence; satyaM = truthfulness; akrodhaH = freedom from anger; tyaagaH = renunciation; shaantiH = tranquillity; apaishunaM = aversion to fault-finding; dayaa = mercy; bhuuteshhu = towards all living entities; aloluptvaM = freedom from greed;

maardavaM = gentleness; hriiH = modesty; achaapalaM = determination.

Nonviolence, truthfulness, absence of anger, renunciation, equanimity, abstaining from malicious talk, compassion for all creatures, freedom from greed, gentleness, modesty, absence of fickleness; (16.02)

तेजः क्षमा धृतिः शौचमद्रोहो नातिमानिता ।
भवन्ति सम्पदं दैवीमभिजातस्य भारत ||१६- ३||

tejaH kShamA dhR^itiH shauchamadroho nAtimAnitA .
bhavanti sampadaM daivImabhijAtasya bhArata .. 16\-3..

tejaH = vigor; kshamaa = forgiveness; dhR^itiH = fortitude; shauchaM = cleanliness; adrohaH = freedom from envy; na = not; ati maanitaa = expectation of honor; bhavanti = are; sampadaM = the qualities; daiviiM = divine nature; abhijaatasya = of one who is born of; bhaarata = O son of Bharata.

Splendor, forgiveness, fortitude, cleanliness, absence of malice, and absence of pride; these are the qualities of those endowed with divine virtues, O Arjuna. (16.03)

दम्भो दर्पोऽभिमानश्च क्रोधः पारुष्यमेव च ।
अज्ञानं चाभिजातस्य पार्थ सम्पदमासुरीम् ||१६- ४||

dambho darpo.abhimAnashcha krodhaH pAruShyameva cha .
aGYAna.n chAbhijAtasya pArtha sampadamAsurIm.h .. 16\-4..

dambhaH = pride; darpaH = arrogance; abhimanaH = conceit; cha = and; krodhaH = anger; paarushhyaM = harshness; eva = certainly; cha = and; aGYaanaM = ignorance; cha = and; abhijaatasya = of one who is born of; paartha = O son of Pritha; sampadaM = the qualities; aasuriiM = the demoniac nature.

Hypocrisy, arrogance, pride, anger, harshness, and ignorance; these are the marks of those who are born with demonic qualities, O Arjuna. (16.04)

दैवी सम्पद्विमोक्षाय निबन्धायासुरी मता ।
मा शुचः सम्पदं दैवीमभिजातोऽसि पाण्डव ||१६- ५||

daivI sampadvimokShAya nibandhAyAsurI matA .

mA shuchaH sampadaM daivImabhijAto.asi pANDava .. 16\-5..

daivii = Divine; sampat.h = assets; vimokshaaya = meant for liberation; nibandhaaya = for bondage; aasurii = demoniac qualities; mataa = are considered; maa = do not; shuchaH = worry; sampadaM = assets; daiviiM = transcendental; abhijaataH = born of; asi = you are; paaNDava = O son of Pandu.

Divine qualities lead to nirvana, the demonic (qualities) are said to be for bondage. Do not grieve, O Arjuna, you are born with divine qualities. (16.05)

द्वौ भूतसर्गौ लोकेऽस्मिन्दैव आसुर एव च ।
दैवो विस्तरशः प्रोक्त आसुरं पार्थ मे शृणु ॥१६- ६॥
dvau bhUtasargau loke.asmindaiva Asura eva cha .
daivo vistarashaH prokta AsuraM pArtha me shR^iNu .. 16\-6..

dvau = two; bhuutasargau = created living beings; loke = in the world; asmin.h = this; daivaH = godly; aasuraH = demoniac; eva = certainly; cha = and; daivaH = the divine; vistarashaH = at great lengt; proktaH = said; aasuraM = the demoniac; paartha = O son of Pritha; me = from Me; shR^iNu = just hear.

There are two types of human beings in this world: the divine, and the demonic. The divine has been described at length, now hear from Me about the demonic, O Arjuna. (16.06)

प्रवृत्तिं च निवृत्तिं च जना न विदुरासुराः ।
न शौचं नापि चाचारो न सत्यं तेषु विद्यते ॥१६- ७॥
pravR^itti.n cha nivR^itti.n cha janA na vidurAsurAH .
na shauchaM nApi chAchAro na satya.n teShu vidyate .. 16\-7..

pravR^ittiM = acting properly; cha = also; nivR^ittiM = not acting improperly; cha = and; janaaH = persons; na = never; viduH = know; aasuraH = of demoniac quality; na = never; shauchaM = cleanliness; na = nor; api = also; cha = and; aachaaraH = behaviour; na = never; satyaM = truth; teshhu = in them; vidyate = there is.

Persons of demonic nature do not know what to do and what not to do. They neither have purity nor good conduct nor truthfulness. (16.07)

असत्यमप्रतिष्ठं ते जगदाहुरनीश्वरम् ।
अपरस्परसम्भूतं किमन्यत्कामहैतुकम् ॥१६- ८॥
asatyamapratiShTha.n te jagadAhuranIshvaram.h .
aparasparasambhUtaM kimanyatkAmahaitukam.h .. 16\-8..

asatyaM = unreal; apratishhThaM = without foundation; te = they; jagat.h = the cosmic manifestation; aahuH = say; aniishvaraM = with no controller; aparaspara = without cause; sambhuutaM = arisen kim; anyat.h = there is no other cause; kaamahaitukaM = it is due to lust only.

They say that the world is without truth, without a substratum, without a God, and brought about by mutual union and is caused by lust (or Kaama) alone and nothing else. (16.08)

एतां दृष्टिमवष्टभ्य नष्टात्मानोऽल्पबुद्धयः ।
प्रभवन्त्युग्रकर्माणः क्षयाय जगतोऽहिताः ॥१६- ९॥
etA.n dR^iShTimavaShTabhya naShTAtmAno.alpabuddhayaH .
prabhavantyugrakarmANaH kShayAya jagato.ahitAH .. 16\-9..

etaaM = this; dR^ishhTiM = vision; avashhTabhya = accepting; nashhTa = having lost; aatmanaH = themselves; alpabuddhayaH = the less intelligent; prabhavanti = flourish; ugrakarmaaNaH = engaged in painful activities; kshayaaya = for destruction; jagataH = of the world; ahitaaH = unbeneficial.

Adhering to this view having lost themselves, with small intellect and cruel deeds, are born as enemies for the destruction of the world. (16.09)

काममाश्रित्य दुष्पूरं दम्भमानमदान्विताः ।
मोहाद्गृहीत्वासद्ग्राहान्प्रवर्तन्तेऽशुचिव्रताः ॥१६- १०॥
kAmamAshritya duShpUraM dambhamAnamadAnvitAH .
mohAd.hgR^ihItvAsad.hgrAhAnpravartante.ashuchivratAH .. 16\-10..

kaamaM = lust; aashritya = taking shelter of; dushhpuuraM = insatiable; dambha = of pride; mana = and false prestige;

madaanvitaaH = absorbed in the conceit; mohaat.h = by illusion; gR^ihiitvaa = taking; asat.h = nonpermanent; graahaan.h = things; pravartante = they flourish; ashuchi = to the unclean; vrataaH = avowed.

Filled with insatiable desires, hypocrisy, pride, and arrogance; holding wrong views due to delusion; they act with impure motives. (16.10)

चिन्तामपरिमेयां च प्रलयान्तामुपाश्रिताः ।
कामोपभोगपरमा एतावदिति निश्चिताः ॥१६- ११॥
chintAmaparimeyA.n cha pralayAntAmupAshritAH .
kAmopabhogaparamA etAvaditi nishchitAH .. 16\-11..

chintaaM = fears and anxieties; aparimeyaM = immeasurable; cha = and; pralayaantaaM = unto the point of death; upaashritaaH = having taken shelter of; kaamopabhoga = sense gratification; paramaaH = the highest goal of life; etaavat.h = thus; iti = in this way; nishchitaaH = having ascertained.

Obsessed with great anxiety until death, considering sense gratification as their highest aim, convinced that this (sense pleasure) is everything, (16.11)

आशापाशशतैर्बद्धाः कामक्रोधपरायणाः ।
ईहन्ते कामभोगार्थमन्यायेनार्थसञ्चयान् ॥१६- १२॥
AshApAshashatairbaddhAH kAmakrodhaparAyaNAH .
Ihante kAmabhogArthamanyAyenArthasa~nchayAn.h .. 16\-12..

aashaapaasha = entanglements in a network of hope; shataiH = by hundreds; baddhaaH = being bound; kaama = of lust; krodha = and anger; paraayaNaaH = always situated in the mentality; iihante = they desire; kaama = lust; bhoga = sense enjoyment; arthaM = for the purpose of; anyaayena = illegally; artha = of wealth; saJNchayaan.h = accumulation.

Bound by hundreds of ties of desire and enslaved by lust and anger; they strive to obtain wealth by unlawful means for the fulfilment of desires. (16.12)

इदमद्य मया लब्धमिमं प्राप्स्ये मनोरथम् ।
इदमस्तीदमपि मे भविष्यति पुनर्धनम् ॥१६- १३॥
idamadya mayA labdhamimaM prApsye manoratham.h .
idamastIdamapi me bhaviShyati punardhanam.h .. 16\-13..

idaM = this; adya = today; mayaa = by me; labdhaM = gained; imaM = this; praapsye = I shall gain; manorathaM = according to my desires; idaM = this; asti = there is; idaM = this; api = also; me = mine; bhavishhyati = it will; increase in the future; punaH = again; dhanaM = wealth.

This has been gained by me today, I shall fulfil this desire, this is mine and this wealth also shall be mine in the future; (16.13)

असौ मया हतः शत्रुर्हनिष्ये चापरानपि ।
ईश्वरोऽहमहं भोगी सिद्धोऽहं बलवान्सुखी ॥१६- १४॥

asau mayA hataH shatrurhaniShye chAparAnapi .
Ishvaro.ahamahaM bhogI siddho.ahaM balavAnsukhI .. 16\-14..

asau = that; mayaa = by me; hataH = has been killed; shatruH = enemy; hanishhye = I shall kill; cha = also; aparaan.h = others; api = certainly; ishvaraH = the lord; ahaM = I am; ahaM = I am; bhogii = the enjoyer; siddhaH = perfect; ahaM = I am; balavaan.h = powerful; sukhii = happy.

That enemy has been slain by me, and I shall slay others also. I am the Lord. I am the enjoyer. I am successful, powerful, and happy; (16.14)

आढ्योऽभिजनवानस्मि कोऽन्योऽस्ति सदृशो मया ।
यक्ष्ये दास्यामि मोदिष्य इत्यज्ञानविमोहिताः ॥१६- १५॥

ADhyo.abhijanavAnasmi ko.anyo.asti sadR^isho mayA .
yakShye dAsyAmi modiShya ityaGYAnavimohitAH .. 16\-15..

aaDhyaH = wealthy; abhijanavaan.h = surrounded by aristocratic relatives; asmi = I am; kaH = who; anyaH = other; asti = there is; sadR^ishaH = like; mayaa = me; yakshye = I shall sacrifice; daasyaami = I shall give charity; modishhye = I shall rejoice; iti = thus; aGYaana = by ignorance; vimohitaaH = deluded.

I am rich and born in a noble family. I am the greatest. I shall perform sacrifice, I shall give charity, and I shall rejoice. Thus deluded by ignorance; (16.15)

अनेकचित्तविभ्रान्ता मोहजालसमावृताः ।
प्रसक्ताः कामभोगेषु पतन्ति नरकेऽशुचौ ॥१६- १६॥

anekachittavibhrAntA mohajAlasamAvR^itAH .
prasaktAH kAmabhogeShu patanti narake.ashuchau .. 16\-16..

aneka = numerous; chitta = by anxieties; vibhraantaaH = perplexed; moha = of illusions; jaala = by a network; samaavR^itaH = surrounded; prasaktaaH = attached; kaamabhogeshhu = to sense gratification; patanti = they glide down; narake = into hell; ashuchau = unclean.

Bewildered by many fancies; entangled in the net of delusion; addicted to the enjoyment of sensual pleasures; they fall into a foul hell. (16.16)

आत्मसम्भाविताः स्तब्धा धनमानमदान्विताः ।
यजन्ते नामयज्ञैस्ते दम्भेनाविधिपूर्वकम् ॥१६- १७॥
AtmasambhAvitAH stabdhA dhanamAnamadAnvitAH .
yajante nAmayaGYaiste dambhenAvidhipUrvakam.h .. 16\-17..

aatmaasambhavitaaH = self-complacent; stabdhaH = impudent; dhanamaana = of wealth and false prestige; mada = in the delusion; anvitaaH = absorbed; yajante = they perform sacrifice; naama = in name only; yaGYaiH = with; sacrifices; te = they; dambhena = out of pride; avidhipuurvakaM = without following any rules and regulations.

Self-conceited, stubborn, filled with pride and intoxication of wealth; they perform Yajna only in name, for show, and not according to scriptural injunction. (16.17)

अहंकारं बलं दर्पं कामं क्रोधं च संश्रिताः ।
मामात्मपरदेहेषु प्रद्विषन्तोऽभ्यसूयकाः ॥१६- १८॥
aha.nkAraM balaM darpa.n kAmaM krodha.n cha sa.nshritAH .
mAmAtmaparadeheShu pradviShanto.abhyasUyakAH .. 16\-18..

ahaN^kaaraM = false ego; balaM = strength; darpaM = pride; kaamaM = lust; krodhaM = anger; cha = also; sa.nshritaaH = having taken shelter of; maaM = Me; aatma = in their own; para = and in other; deheshhu = bodies; pradvishhantaH = blaspheming; abhyasuuyakaaH = envious.

Clinging to egoism, power, arrogance, lust, and anger; these malicious people hate Me (who dwells) in their own body and others' bodies. (16.18)

तानहं द्विषतः क्रुरान्संसारेषु नराधमान् ।
क्षिपाम्यजस्रमशुभानासुरीष्वेव योनिषु ॥१६- १९॥
tAnahaM dviShataH krurAnsa.nsAreShu narAdhamAn.h .
kShipAmyajasramashubhAnAsurIShveva yoniShu .. 16\-
19..

taan.h = those; ahaM = I; dvishhataH = envious; kruuraan.h = mischievous; sa.nsaareshhu = into the ocean of; material existence; naraadhamaan.h = the lowest of mankind; kshipaami = I put; ajasraM = forever; ashubhaan.h = inauspicious; aasuriishhu = demoniac; eva = certainly; yonishhu = into the wombs.

I hurl these haters, cruel, sinful, and mean people of the world, into the wombs of demons again and again. (16.19)

आसुरीं योनिमापन्ना मूढा जन्मनि जन्मनि ।
मामप्राप्यैव कौन्तेय ततो यान्त्यधमां गतिम् ॥१६- २०॥
AsurI.n yonimApannA mUDhA janmani janmani .
mAmaprApyaiva kaunteya tato yAntyadhamA.n gatim.h ..
16\-20..

aasuriiM = demoniac; yoniM = species; aapannaaH = gaining; muuDhaaH = the foolish; janmani janmani = in birth after birth; maaM = Me; apraapya = without achieving; eva = certainly; kaunteya = O son of Kunti; tataH = thereafter; yaanti = go; adhamaaM = condemned; gatiM = destination.

O Arjuna, entering the wombs of demons birth after birth, the deluded ones sink to the lowest hell without ever attaining Me. (16.20)

त्रिविधं नरकस्येदं द्वारं नाशनमात्मनः ।
कामः क्रोधस्तथा लोभस्तस्मादेतत्त्रयं त्यजेत् ॥१६- २१॥
trividhaM narakasyedaM dvAraM nAshanamAtmanaH .
kAmaH krodhastathA lobhastasmAdetattrayaM tyajet.h ..
16\-21..

trividhaM = of three kinds; narakasya = of hell; idaM = this; dvaaraM = gate; naashanaM = destructive; aatmanaH = of the self; kaamaH = lust; krodhaH = anger; tathaa = as well as; lobhaH =

greed; tasmaat.h = therefore; etat.h = these; trayaM = three; tyajet.h = one must give up.

Lust, anger, and greed are the three gates of hell leading to the downfall (or bondage). Therefore, one must (learn to) give up these three. (16.21)

एतैर्विमुक्तः कौन्तेय तमोद्वारैस्त्रिभिर्नरः ।
आचरत्यात्मनः श्रेयस्ततो याति परां गतिम् ॥१६- २२॥
etairvimuktaH kaunteya tamodvAraistribhirnaraH .
AcharatyAtmanaH shreyastato yAti parAM gatim.h .. 16\-22..

etaiH = from these; vimuktaH = being liberated; kaunteya = O son of Kunti; tamodvaaraiH = from the gates of; ignorance; tribhiH = of three kinds; naraH = a person; aacharati = performs; aatmanaH = for the self; shreyaH = benediction; tataH = thereafter; yaati = he goes; paraaM = to the supreme; gatiM = destination.

One who is liberated from these three gates of hell, O Arjuna, does what is best, and attains the supreme goal. (16.22)

यः शास्त्रविधिमुत्सृज्य वर्तते कामकारतः ।
न स सिद्धिमवाप्नोति न सुखं न परां गतिम् ॥१६- २३॥
yaH shAstravidhimutsR^ijya vartate kAmakArataH .
na sa siddhimavApnoti na sukhaM na parAM gatim.h .. 16\-23..

yaH = anyone who; shaastravidhiM = the regulations of the scriptures; utsR^ijya = giving up; vartate = remains; kaamakaarataH = acting whimsically in lust; na = never; saH = he; siddhiM = perfection; avaapnoti = achieves; na = never; sukhaM = happiness; na = never; paraaM = the supreme; gatiM = perfectional stage.

One who acts under the influence of their desires, disobeying scriptural injunctions, neither attains perfection nor happiness nor the supreme goal. (16.23)

तस्माच्छास्त्रं प्रमाणं ते कार्याकार्यव्यवस्थितौ ।
ज्ञात्वा शास्त्रविधानोक्तं कर्म कर्तुमिहार्हसि ॥१६- २४॥

tasmAchchhAstraM pramANaM te kAryAkAryavyavasthitau .
GYAtvA shAstravidhAnokta.n karma kartumihArhasi .. 16\-24..

tasmaat.h = therefore; shaastraM = the scriptures; pramaaNaM = evidence; te = your; kaarya = duty; akaarya = and forbidden activities; vyavasthitau = in determining; GYaatvaa = knowing; shaastra = of scripture; vidhaana = the regulations; uktaM = as declared; karma = work; kartuM = do; iha = in this world; arhasi = you should.

Therefore, let the scripture be your authority in determining what should be done and what should not be done. You should perform your duty following the scriptural injunction. (16.24)

ॐ तत्सदिति श्रीमद्भगवद्गीतासूपनिषत्सु
ब्रह्मविद्यायां योगशास्त्रे श्रीकृष्णार्जुनसंवादे
दैवासुरसम्पद्विभागयोगो नाम षोडशोऽध्यायः ॥१६॥

AUM tatsaditi shrImadbhagavadgItAsUpaniShatsu
brahmavidyAyA.n yogashAstre shrIkR^iShNArjunasa.nvAde
daivAsurasampadvibhAgayogo nAma ShoDasho.adhyAyaH .. 16..
\

17. Three Kinds of Faith

"According to the trend of our desires and the nature of our souls, each one of us generally becomes of a corresponding character." –Plato (Laws-[904c])

Introduction

The scriptures teach us the secrets of knowledge and wisdom that forms the foundation to guide our actions. In the verse 16.24, Lord advises taking refuge in scriptures as they guide us about actions, intentions and methods that foster composure and serenity. Arjun got an opportunity to ask the following question.

Those who worship, casting aside the advice of the scriptures, but with full faith, -- how is their state? Is it sattva, rajas or tamas?

Only the Scriptures teach us the art of involvement without entanglement. Nature, consisting of the three attributes (Trigun) binds those who do not understand that secret art. According to one's nature, altruism, passion or lethargy is one's guiding force. The corresponding Sattvik, Rajasik and Tamasik Gunas bind the practitioner to this world.

Shraddha or faith is one of an essential element of that art, but faith alone, without the mystical knowledge of the scriptures, cannot liberate one from the fruit of his action. Unless one understands that the invisible, formless, eternal Supreme is the only truth, and is aware of this (AUM TAT SAT) while doing every action including sacrifice, austerity and charity, the actions bind one to the fruit of such acts and the subject cannot liberate. Answers to this general question about the importance of faith and the knowledge of the scriptures, with several particular references, constitute the teachings of this chapter.

Chapter Summary:

Those who set aside the advice of the scriptures or those who have not studied them are unaware of the knowledge enshrined in them. The worship of such an unaware person is of three kinds:- sattva, rajas and tamas. The Saattvika persons worship Devas, the Raajasika people worship Yaksha and Rakshasa, and the Taamasika persons worship ghosts and spirits.

Ignorant of the wisdom of the scriptures, they perform gruesome austerities. Hypocrisy and egotism is their driving force. Unintelligently torturing the elements in their body and also the Supreme who dwells within their body, these ignorant people are certainly demonic.

Choices, likings, worship, charities, and austerities of the people unaware of the secret knowledge of the scriptures depend on their Gunas (attributes) and hence the results of those acts and choices bind them to the result of their actions.

Elaborating on the food preferences of the people with Sattvik Gunas (superior qualities) Lord says that such people are fond of juicy, smooth, substantial, and food that is agreeable to the stomach. These food items *promote longevity, virtue, strength, health, happiness, and joy.*

Food items preferred by passionate people are bitter, sour, salty, very hot, pungent, dry, and burning and cause pain, grief, and disease. Further, discussing the food items favoured by Tamasiks, Lord says, such people like food that is half-cooked, tasteless, rotten, stale, abandoned, and impure.

Further, Lord proceeds to describe three kinds of sacrifices. The Satvik sacrifice is according to the laid down procedures, performed with a firm belief that it is a duty, and without the desire for the fruit. The Rajasik sacrifice is for fruit and self-glorification and the Tamasik sacrifice is contrary to the scriptures, devoid of faith, resolution and welfare.

Respect or worship of Dev, the educated, teacher and wise; purity, simplicity, brahmacharya, and nonviolence are the austerities of deeds. Speech that is not offensive, truthful, pleasant, beneficial, and which is used for regular reading of scriptures is the austerity of speech. The serenity of mind, gentleness, silence, self-restraint and the purity of mind is the austerity of thought.

Threefold austerity of thought, word, and deed practised by yogis with supreme faith, without a desire for the fruit, is said to be Saattvika austerity. The one that is done for gaining respect, honour, reverence, and for show-off, is said to be Raajasika, unsteady, and impermanent. And that austerity, which is performed without proper understanding, or with self-torture, or for harming others, is Taamasika austerity.

The charity that is given as a matter of duty, to a deserving candidate who does nothing in return, at the right place and time, is called a Saattvika charity. That, which is given unwillingly, or to get something in return, or looking for some fruit, is called Raajasika charity. The one, that is given at the wrong place and time, to unworthy persons, without paying respect or with contempt, is said to be Taamasika charity.

"OM TAT SAT" is said to be the threefold name of Brahm. The Brahmana, the Vedas, and the Yajna were created from this in ancient time. Therefore, acts of sacrifice, charity, and austerity prescribed in the scriptures are always commenced by uttering "OM" by the knowers of Brahm.

Various types of sacrifice, charity, and austerity are performed by the seekers of nirvana by uttering "TAT" (or He is all) without seeking a reward. SAT is used in the sense of reality and goodness. The word "SAT" is also used for an auspicious act. Steadfastness in sacrifice, charity, and austerity is also called "SAT". The action for the sake of the Supreme is verily termed as "SAT". Whatever is done without faith; whether it is sacrifice, charity, austerity, or any other act; is called Asat. It has no value here or hereafter, say Lord Krishna.

Key Terms:

shraddha: (**श्रद्धा; Itrans** ; Itrans: shraddhA) The term is derived from two Sanskrit roots: "*shrat*" meaning "truth," "heart" or "faithfulness," and "*dhaa*", meaning "to direct one's mind toward." As such, shraddha can be understood to reflect the virtues, values and inner self of a person. It may also be interpreted as a firmly held conviction in the life path that an individual has chosen. As a philosophical concept, shraddha differs from the Western idea of faith, in that it refers to a direct understanding of Divine truth, rather than belief through blind faith. It refers to a concept similar to faith, drive or purpose. Although it does not have a direct English translation, it describes a type of positive energy that comes from deep within a person, shaping their world and life. Like other scholars, we also translate it as faith, conviction or belief but one must understand that it is a loose translation.

Yajante: (**यजन्ते** ; **itrans:** yajante): It is derived from root word yaj, which means to worship, adore, honour (especially with oblations). It is the act of performing yagya or yajana. Yajante here in this chapter refers to of worship, veneration or adoration. It also metamorphically refers to the action. Also here in Gita, the yajna is not same as the ceremonial sacrifice of the Veda. It is sacrificial action and services, where one dedicates his selfless deeds and services to the service of the Supreme existing as the common life force of all beings.

Pret: (**प्रेत** ; **itrans**: pret): the dead, or their spirit, those who have departed.

Bhoot: (**भूत** ; **itrans:** bhoota); been, gone, past, or a spirit (good or evil), the ghost of a deceased person, a demon.

Brahmana: (**ब्राह्मण**; **itrans** : braahma.na) The Brahmana are the part of Vedic literature that contain rules for the employment of the Mantras or hymns at various sacrifices, with detailed explanations of their origin and meaning and numerous old legends.

Analysis:

Those Full of Faith are Guided by their Nature:

You may recall that in 16.23 and 16.24 Lord says that those who set aside the ordinance of scriptures, follow the promptings of their desires do not attain perfection, happiness or the highest goal. Therefore, let the doctrine of the scriptures be your guide in determining the right conduct.

Prompted by the advice of the Lord to follow the scriptures, Arjuna found it suitable to raise his doubt about the conduct which is full of Shraddha (faith), but not according to the sacred teachings. Lord begin to elucidate that in such cases the faith of such individuals, if not guided by the scriptural injunction, is controlled by their nature, which can be Satvik, Rajasik or Tamasik.

Further, emphasizing the importance of faith, Lord says that a person is what his faith is. The nature of each individual plays a vital role in shaping their convictions. These beliefs are so powerful that they can salvage a person and can also take his life.

To illustrate the concept, please refer to a paper titled "Voodoo death" by famous American physiologist Walter Cannon, published in 1942. Cannon, based on a thorough search of reports from many primitive societies concluded that the phenomenon of voodoo deaths is characteristically noted among aboriginals—among human beings so primitive, so superstitious and ignorant, that they feel bewildered strangers in a hostile world. Instead of knowledge, their fertile and unrestricted imaginations fill their environment with all sort of evil spirits capable of affecting their lives disastrously.

CURT P. RICHTER, another outstanding psychobiologist, carried out some interesting experiments on rats to understand this phenomenon further. In his path-breaking paper titled "On the Phenomenon of Sudden Death in Animals and Man" published in 1950, he describes an experiment where he put rats into large buckets, half-filled with circulating water. The rats lasted about fifteen minutes before giving up and succumbing to the depths of the bucket.

In a follow-up experiment, before the rats started to succumb and sink, he pulled the drowning rodents to safety, dried them off, gave them a brief period of rest only to put them right back into that same bucket and repeated this process a few times. Here comes the amazing part – those same rats now swam for an average of sixty *hours.* Richter concluded that saving a rat from drowning – even temporarily, gave that rat *hope.* Since the rats **believed or had faith** that they would finally be rescued, they could push their bodies way beyond what they previously thought impossible.

A pearl of similar wisdom is reflected in Plato's famous work "Laws" where he states that each one of us develops a character according to the trend of our desires and the nature of our souls.

Right faith or belief is therefore very critical in the progress and survival of an individual. In the absence of scriptural knowledge, individual nature will be the guiding factor in the development of the faith of such persons, which may not be the optimum alternative. Lord describes this by examples elaborating objects of worship, food choices, austerity, and charity of such people under the influence of their nature but unaware of the wisdom of the scriptures.

Worship by the three categories of people:

Thereafter, Lord continues to describe the objects of worship of diverse types of people. The people with Satvik nature worship Gods, whereas those with Rajasik character worship gnomes and giants. Those with Tamasik personality worship the dead and their spirits.

Desire and passion, not the scriptural injunction, is the force behind their severe austerities. Tormenting all the elements in their body and the Lord who dwells within, they are stupid and demonic in their resolve.

Three kinds of people and their choices regarding food, worship, austerity and charity :

Food:

The nature of a person, Satvik, Rajasik, or Tamasik also determines their food choices, as well as worship, austerity and charity. The foods which increase vitality, vigour, strength, health, joy and cheerfulness, and are savoury and oleaginous, satiating for a longer time, substantial and agreeable, are dear to the Sattvic. Cuisine with bitter, sour, saline, taste; and excessively hot, pungent, dry, and burning; which cause pain, grief, and sickness; are cherished by Raajasika persons. Tamasiks like the foodstuff that is stale and flat, putrid and corrupt leftover and unclean.

Worship (Deeds):

Here the word Yagya has been used figuratively to indicate deeds performed by an individual.

Desiring no fruit, while performing their actions with a fixed resolve in mind that they should merely perform their tasks selflessly, as explained in the scriptures is Satvik. Performed to fulfil their desires and for self-glorification, such acts are defined as Rajasik.

The work performed while disobeying the applicable laws, without paying the dues to the participants/ workers, without giving applicable credits to the team and also without sharing the outcome of the work with the society is termed as Tamasik in nature.

Even if we consider the literal meaning of the Yagya as worship, the worship without any desire for fruit is considered Satvik, the prayer to fulfil desires and for self-glorification is regarded Rajasik and the one without following scriptural methods, devoid of the Mantras, and faith is considered Tamasik.

Austerities of Body, Speech, and Mind:

Austerities are efforts to improve oneself. They are of three types – austerities of body, speech and mind.

Knowledge had the highest regard in Vedic civilization and those associated with knowledge work were regarded in high esteem including teachers, and students. The day of commencement of the formal education was celebrated as the second birthday and those who had undergone formal education were called Dwij or twice-born.

Worshipping the God, the twice-borns, the teachers and the wise men are part of the austerity of the body. Further, maintaining a clean body, uprightness, trading the path to reach the abode of the supreme, and nonviolence is also penance of the body. The knowledge of the scriptures was transmitted through oral recitation in those days under the guidance of the teacher. It had several advantages over written transmission such as:

Srutis contained texts having deep philosophical meaning. The teacher, while transmitting the text orally would also act as an interpreter of those texts. Additionally, it also eliminated the chances of corruption, often incorporated while transferring the knowledge through written words.

The era of those manuscripts was not the age of the printing press. The written material was often handwritten, and therefore, the number of written copies were limited. For important works such as sruti, it would have been more secure to preserve the knowledge through oral tradition, as it was a safer bet. Handwritten literature had the danger of extinction due to attacks or natural disasters.

Due to the facts brought out above, the speech was the medium of study of scriptures. The austerity of speech, therefore, consisted of the study of holy books, especially Srutis. It is also the speech that does not annoy and is true, pleasant, and beneficial. This verse accentuates the practice to speak the truth, as well as the words that are pleasant and beneficial and does not annoy anyone.

Maintaining mental happiness is an attribute that requires cerebral efforts. Similarly, gentle behaviour also calls for self-control of the mind. Keeping silence requires constant mind control where one requires to resist the temptation to speak. The purity of intention is honesty while dealing with others. Summarizing the above, mental austerity is the serenity of the mind, gentleness, silence, self-control, and the purity of intention.

The three Kinds of Austerities According to Guna

Lord proceed to elaborate that the three kinds of austerities - bodily, spoken and mental as described in the previous section are of three types according to the nature of an individual.

The austerities performed by devout persons with utmost faith desiring no return are Satvik. Those conducted to gain respect, honour or worship and for ostentation are Rajasik unstable and not lasting. Furthermore, the austerities done under delusion, with self-torture or to destroy another is Tamasik. Following this, Lord describes the threefold nature of giving alms.

Threefold Nature of the Donations:

Alms given to a worthy person from whom no return is expected with a feeling of duty, at a proper time and place where it is useful is called Satvik gift.

For instance, somebody having Satvik qualities will offer donations to a person in need even if he is unknown. He will try to give the donations at a moment and time when it is most desirable.

People having Rajasik properties give alms with the intention of return at a later date. Giving donations looking for a future gain or with reluctance is a sign of Rajasik qualities.

The charity given to an unworthy person, at an inappropriate time and place is Tamasik in nature. The purpose of donations is to help those in dire need. One should choose the right person or institution for greater impact. Also, the time and place of the charity have their influence on the effectiveness of the beneficiation.

To illustrate the importance of the right time, place and worthiness of a person to whom charity is given, let us take an example of a natural calamity. Help should reach to the affected people at the appropriate time and place either directly or through the agencies involved.

As explained above, people according to their nature perform various sorts of worships, penances, and charities. They get the results of these acts accordingly. However, to evade the trap of karma, these acts shall be performed according to the scriptural injunctions as explained further.

Going Beyond the Three Qualities:

The scriptures tell us the secret of how to go beyond the three attributes(Satvik, Rajasik and Tamasik) and achieve the abode of the Supreme.

The essence of the ancient scriptures, The Veda and the Brahmana, is "AUM TAT SAT". Therefore, the knower of the Eternal begins all the acts of prayer, charity and austerity with the utterance of AUM, says Lord.

AUM is the symbolic representation of the Supreme. It encompasses the whole of the universe- past, present, and future and also the Self residing in all of the beings as declared in the Vedic texts.

Those desiring Moksha or liberation execute all acts of worship, austerity and charity by pronouncing "TAT" and without aiming for the fruit in return. "TAT "is a Sanskrit pronoun indicating towards the Supreme, symbolically represented by AUM. After explaining the use of "AUM" and "TAT", Lord further describes the use of "SAT". "SAT" is used in the sense of "true reality" and "goodness". The word "SAT" is also used for praiseworthy action.

Steadfastness in worship, austerity and charity is called "SAT" and action for the sake of Supreme is also called "SAT". Finally, the Lord completes the answer to Arjuna's question concluding that whatever is offered without faith-- oblation, austerity, alms or deeds, are ASAT or false and are useful neither here nor hereafter.

It is concluded, therefore, that the deeds performed without faith are ineffective.

Further, the acts performed with faith, but without the use of "AUM TAT SAT" as indicated in the scriptures, will also be worthless in this world and beyond. This symbolically implies that unless the actions performed are dedicated to the Supreme without desiring for the results for oneself, will bind one, and will be a hindrance in liberation.

Original Sanskrit with Word Meanings, Transliteration and Translation (Chapter-17)

अथ सप्तदशोऽध्यायः । श्रद्धात्रयविभागयोगः

atha saptadasho.adhyAyaH .
shraddhAtrayavibhAgayogaH
Here begins the Seventeenth chapter
(shraddhAtrayavibhAgayogo)

अर्जुन उवाच ।
ये शास्त्रविधिमुत्सृज्य यजन्ते श्रद्धयान्विताः ।
तेषां निष्ठा तु का कृष्ण सत्त्वमाहो रजस्तमः ॥१७- १॥

arjuna uvAcha .
ye shAstravidhimutsR^ijya yajante shraddhayAnvitAH .
teShA.n niShThA tu kA kR^iShNa sattvamAho rajastamaH .. 17\-1..

arjuna uvaacha = Arjuna said; ye = those who; shaastravidhiM = the regulations of scripture; utsR^ijya = giving up; yajante = worship; shraddhayaa = full faith; anvitaaH = possessed of; teshhaaM = of them; nishhThaa = state; tu = but; kaa = what; kR^ishhNa = O KRishhNa; sattvaM = purity; aaho = or else; rajaH = in passion; tamaH = in ignorance.

Arjuna said: Those abandoning the scriptural directions worship with full faith, how is there state O Krishna? Is it one of purity, passion, or darkness? (17.01)

श्रीभगवानुवाच ।
त्रिविधा भवति श्रद्धा देहिनां सा स्वभावजा ।
सात्त्विकी राजसी चैव तामसी चेति तां शृणु ॥१७- २॥

shrIbhagavAnuvAcha .
trividhA bhavati shraddhA dehinA.n sA svabhAvajA .
sAttvikI rAjasI chaiva tAmasI cheti tA.n shR^iNu .. 17\-2..

shriibhagavaanuvaacha = the blessed Lord said; trividhaa = of three kinds; bhavati = becomes; shraddhaa = the faith; dehinaaM = of the embodied; saa = that; svabhaavajaa = according to his own nature; saattvikii = in the mode of goodness; raajasii = in the mode of passion; cha = also; eva = certainly; taamasii = in the mode of ignorance; cha = and; iti = thus; taaM = that; shR^iNu = hear from Me.

The Supreme Lord said: The natural faith of embodied beings is of three types: pure, passionate and dark. You hear that from me.

सत्त्वानुरूपा सर्वस्य श्रद्धा भवति भारत ।
श्रद्धामयोऽयं पुरुषो यो यच्छ्रद्धः स एव सः ॥१७- ३॥

sattvAnurUpA sarvasya shraddhA bhavati bhArata .
shraddhAmayo.ayaM puruSho yo yachchhraddhaH sa eva saH .. 17\-3..

sattvaanuruupaa = according to the existence; sarvasya = of everyone; shraddhaa = faith; bhavati = becomes; bhaarata = O son of Bharata; shraddhaa = faith; mayaH = full of; ayaM = this; purushhaH = person; yaH = who; yat.h = having which; shraddhaH = faith; saH = thus; eva = certainly; saH = he.

O Arjuna, the faith of each is in accordance with one's own nature. A man consists of his faith, he certainly becomes one according to his faith (17.03)

यजन्ते सात्त्विका देवान्यक्षरक्षांसि राजसाः ।
प्रेतान्भूतगणांश्चान्ये यजन्ते तामसा जनाः ॥१७- ४॥

yajante sAttvikA devAnyakSharakShA.nsi rAjasAH .
pretAnbhUtagaNA.nshchAnye yajante tAmasA janAH .. 17\-4..

yajante = worship; saattvikaaH = pure; devaan.h = the shining one; yaksharakshaa.nsi = yaksh and rakshasa; raajasaaH = passionate; pretaan.h = dead or spirit of deads; bhuutagaNaan.h = ghosts; cha = and; anye = others; yajante = worship; taamasaaH = ignorant; janaaH = people.

The Saattvika persons worship Devas, the Raajasika people worship Yaksha and Rakshasa, and the Taamasika persons worship ghosts and spirits. (17.04)

अशास्त्रविहितं घोरं तप्यन्ते ये तपो जनाः ।
दम्भाहंकारसंयुक्ताः कामरागबलान्विताः ॥१७- ५॥

ashAstravihitaM ghoraM tapyante ye tapo janAH .
dambhAha.nkArasa.nyuktAH kAmarAgabalAnvitAH .. 17\-5..

ashaastra = not in the scriptures; vihitaM = directed; ghoraM = terrible; tapyante = undergo; ye = those who; tapaH = austerities; janaaH = persons; dambha = with pride; ahaN^kaara = and egoism; sa.nyuktaaH = engaged; kaama = of lust; raaga = and attachment; bala = by the force; anvitaaH = filled.

Without following the scriptures, practicing terrible austerities, these people with hypocrisy and egotism, are driven by lust, and attachment; (17.05)

कर्षयन्तः शरीरस्थं भूतग्राममचेतसः ।
मां चैवान्तःशरीरस्थं तान्विद्ध्यासुरनिश्चयान् ||१७- ६||

karShayantaH sharIrasthaM bhUtagrAmamachetasaH .
mA.n chaivAntaHsharIrastha.n tAnvid.hdhyAsuranishchayAn.h .. 17\-6..

karshhayantaH = tormenting; shariirasthaM = situated within the body; bhuutagraamaM = the combination of material elements; achetasaH = unintelligently; maaM = Me; cha = also; eva = certainly; antaH = within; shariirasthaM = situated in the body; taan.h = them; viddhi = understand; aasura; demons; nishchayaan.h = certainly.

unintelligently torturing the elements in their body and also Me who dwell within the body; know these ignorant persons to be of demonic nature. (17.06)

आहारस्त्वपि सर्वस्य त्रिविधो भवति प्रियः ।
यज्ञस्तपस्तथा दानं तेषां भेदमिमं शृणु ||१७- ७||

AhArastvapi sarvasya trividho bhavati priyaH .
yaGYastapastathA dAnaM teShAM bhedamimaM shR^iNu .. 17\-7..

aahaaraH = eating; tu = certainly; api = also; sarvasya = of everyone; trividhaH = of three kinds; bhavati = there is; priyaH = dear; yaGYaH = sacrifice; tapaH = austerity; tathaa = also; daanaM = charity; teshhaaM = of them; bhedaM = the differences; imaM = this; shR^iNu = hear.

The food preferred by all is also of three types. So are the sacrifice, austerity, and charity. Now hear the distinction between them. (17.07)

आयुःसत्त्वबलारोग्यसुखप्रीतिविवर्धनाः ।
रस्याः स्निग्धाः स्थिरा हृद्या आहाराः सात्त्विकप्रियाः ||१७- ८||

AyuHsattvabalArogyasukhaprItivivardhanAH .

rasyAH snigdhAH sthirA hR^idyA AhArAH sAttvikapriyAH .. 17\-8..

aayuH = duration of life; sattva = vitality; bala = strength; aarogya = health; sukha = happiness; priiti = and satisfaction; vivardhanaaH = increasing; rasyaaH = juicy; snigdhaaH = Unctuous ; sthiraaH = enduring; hR^idyaaH = pleasing to the heart; aahaaraH = food; saattvika = to one in goodness; priyaaH = palatable.

The foods that promote longevity, virtue, strength, health, happiness, and joy; are juicy, smooth, substantial, and agreeable to the stomach. Such foods are dear to the Saattvika persons. (17.08)

कट्वम्ललवणात्युष्णतीक्ष्णरूक्षविदाहिनः ।
आहारा राजसस्येष्टा दुःखशोकामयप्रदाः ॥१७- ९॥
kaT.hvamlalavaNAtyuShNatIkShNarUkShavidAhinaH .
AhArA rAjasasyeShTA duHkhashokAmayapradAH .. 17\-
9..

kaTu = bitter; aamla = sour; lavaNa = salty; atyushhNa = very hot; tiikshNa = pungent; ruksha = dry; vidaahinaH = burning; aahaaraH = food; raajasasya = to one in the mode of passion; ishhTaaH = palatable; duHkha = distress; shoka = misery; aamaya = disease; pradaaH = causing.

Foods that are bitter, sour, salty, very hot, pungent, dry, and burning; and cause pain, grief, and disease; are liked by Raajasika persons. (17.09)

यातयामं गतरसं पूति पर्युषितं च यत् ।
उच्छिष्टमपि चामेध्यं भोजनं तामसप्रियम् ॥१७- १०॥
yAtayAmaM gatarasaM pUti paryuShita.n cha yat.h .
uchchhiShTamapi chAmedhyaM bhojanaM tAmasapriyam.h .. 17\-10..

yaatayaamaM = food cooked hours before being eaten; gatarasaM = tasteless; puuti = bad-smelling; paryushhitaM = decomposed; cha = also; yat.h = that which; uchchhishhTaM = remnants of food eaten by others; api = also; cha = and; amedhyaM = unclean; bhojanaM = eating; taamasa = to one in the mode of darkness; priyaM = dear.

The foods liked by Taamasika persons are half-cooked, tasteless, rotten, stale, refuses, and impure (such as meat and alcohol). (17.10)

अफलाङ्क्षिभिर्यज्ञो विधिदृष्टो य इज्यते ।
यष्टव्यमेवेति मनः समाधाय स सात्त्विकः ॥१७- ११॥
aphalAN^kShibhiryaGYo vidhidR^iShTo ya ijyate .
yaShTavyameveti manaH samAdhAya sa sAttvikaH .. 17\-11..

aphalaakaaN^kshibhiH = by those devoid of desire for result; yaGYaH = sacrifice; vidhidishhTaH = according to the direction of scripture; yaH = which; ijyate = is performed; yashhTavyaM = must be performed; eva = certainly; iti = thus; manaH = mind; samaadhaaya = fixing; saH = it; saattvikaH = in the mode of goodness.

Yajna enjoined by the scriptures, performed with a firm belief that it is a duty, and without the desire for the fruit, is Saattvika Yajna. (17.11)

अभिसन्धाय तु फलं दम्भार्थमपि चैव यत् ।
इज्यते भरतश्रेष्ठ तं यज्ञं विद्धि राजसम् ॥१७- १२॥
abhisandhAya tu phalaM dambhArthamapi chaiva yat.h .
ijyate bharatashreShTha taM yaGYa.n viddhi rAjasam.h .. 17\-12..

abhisandhaaya = desiring; tu = but; phalaM = the result; dambha = pride; arthaM = for the sake of; api = also; cha = and; eva = certainly; yat.h = that which; ijyate = is performed; bharatashreshhTha = O chief of the Bharatas; taM = that; yaGYaM = sacrifice; viddhi = know; raajasaM = in the mode of passion.

Yajna which is performed only for show, or aiming for fruit, know that to be Raajasika Yajna, O Arjuna. (17.12)

विधिहीनमसृष्टान्नं मन्त्रहीनमदक्षिणम् ।
श्रद्धाविरहितं यज्ञं तामसं परिचक्षते ॥१७- १३॥
vidhihInamasR^iShTAnnaM mantrahInamadakShiNam.h .
shraddhAvirahitaM yaGYa.n tAmasaM parichakShate .. 17\-13..

vidhihiinaM = without scriptural direction; asR^ishhTaannaM = without distribution of prasaadam; mantrahiinaM = with no chanting of the Vedic hymns; adakshiNaM = with no remunerations to the priests; shraddhaa = faith; virahitaM = without; yaGYaM = sacrifice; taamasaM = in the mode of ignorance; parichakshate = is to be considered.

Yajna that is performed without following the scripture, in which no food is distributed, which is devoid of mantra, faith, and gift, is said to be Taamasika Yajna. (17.13)

देवद्विजगुरुप्राज्ञपूजनं शौचमार्जवम् ।
ब्रह्मचर्यमहिंसा च शारीरं तप उच्यते ॥१७- १४॥

devadvijaguruprAGYapUjanaM shauchamArjavam.h .
brahmacharyamahi.nsA cha shArIraM tapa uchyate .. 17\-14..

deva = of the Supreme Lord; dvija = the twice born; guru = the spiritual master; praGYaa = and worshipable personalities; puujaanaM = worship/ respect; shauchaM = cleanliness; aarjavaM = simplicity; brahmacharyaM = celibacy; ahi.nsaa = nonviolence; cha = also; shariiraM = pertaining to the body; tapaH = austerity; uchyate = is said to be.

The respect/ worship of Devas, twice-born, guru, and the wise; purity, simplicity, celibacy, and nonviolence; these are said to be the austerity of deed. (17.14)

अनुद्वेगकरं वाक्यं सत्यं प्रियहितं च यत् ।
स्वाध्यायाभ्यसनं चैव वाङ्मयं तप उच्यते ॥१७- १५॥

anudvegakaraM vAkya.n satyaM priyahita.n cha yat.h .
svAdhyAyAbhyasana.n chaiva vAN^mayaM tapa uchyate .. 17\-15..

anudvegakaraM = not agitating; vaakyaM = words; satyaM = truthful; priya = dear; hitaM = beneficial; cha = also; yat.h = which; svaadhyaaya = of Vedic study; abhyasanaM = practice; cha = also; eva = certainly; vaaN^mayaM = of the voice; tapaH = austerity;uchyate = is said to be.

Speech that is not offensive, truthful, pleasant, beneficial, and is used for the regular reading of scriptures is called the austerity of word. (17.15)

मनः प्रसादः सौम्यत्वं मौनमात्मविनिग्रहः ।
भावसंशुद्धिरित्येतत्तपो मानसमुच्यते ॥१७- १६॥
manaH prasAdaH saumyatvaM maunamAtmavinigrahaH .
bhAvasa.nshuddhirityetattapo mAnasamuchyate .. 17\-16..

manaHprasaadaH = satisfaction of the mind; saumyatvaM = being without duplicity towards others; maunaM = gravity; aatma = of the self; vinigrahaH = control; bhaava = of one's intention; sa.nshuddhiH = purification; iti = thus; etat.h = this; tapaH = austerity; maanasaM = of the mind; uchyate = is said to be.

The serenity of mind, gentleness, silence, self-restraint, and the purity of intent are called the austerity of thought. (17.16)

श्रद्धया परया तप्तं तपस्तत्त्रिविधं नरैः ।
अफलाकाङ्क्षिभिर्युक्तैः सात्त्विकं परिचक्षते ॥१७- १७॥
shraddhayA parayA tapta.n tapastattrividhaM naraiH .
aphalAkAN^kShibhiryuktaiH sAttvikaM parichakShate .. 17\-17..

shraddhayaa = with faith; parayaa = great; taptaM = executed; tapaH = austerity; tat.h = that; trividhaM = of three kinds; naraiH = by men; aphalaakaaN^kshibhiH = who are without desires for fruits; yuktaiH = engaged; saattvikaM = in the mode of goodness; parichakshate = is called.

Threefold austerity (of thought, word, and deed) practiced by yogis with supreme faith, without a desire for the fruit, is said to be Saattvika austerity. (17.17)

सत्कारमानपूजार्थं तपो दम्भेन चैव यत् ।
क्रियते तदिह प्रोक्तं राजसं चलमध्रुवम् ॥१७- १८॥
satkAramAnapUjArtha.n tapo dambhena chaiva yat.h .
kriyate tadiha prokta.n rAjasa.n chalamadhruvam.h .. 17\-18..

satkaara = respect; maana = honor; puujaa = and worship; arthaM = for the sake of; tapaH = austerity; dambhena = with pride; cha = also; eva = certainly; yat.h = which; kriyate = is performed; tat.h = that; iha = in this world; proktaM = is said; raajasaM = in the mode of passion; chalaM = flickering; adhruvaM = temporary.

Austerity that is done for gaining respect, honor, reverence, and for show, is said to be Raajasika, unsteady, and impermanent. (17.18)

मूढग्राहेणात्मनो यत्पीडया क्रियते तपः ।
परस्योत्सादनार्थं वा तत्तामसमुदाहृतम् ॥१७- १९॥

mUDhagrAheNAtmano yatpIDayA kriyate tapaH .
parasyotsAdanArtha.n vA tattAmasamudAhR^itam.h .. 17\-19..

muuDha = foolish; graaheNa = with endeavour; aatmanaH = of one's own self; yat.h = which; piiDayaa = by torture; kriyate = is performed; tapaH = penance; parasya = to others; utsaadanaarthaM = for the sake of causing annihilation; vaa = or; tat.h = that; taamasaM = in the mode of darkness; udaahR^itaM = is said to be.

Austerity performed without proper understanding, or with self-torture, or for harming others, is declared as Taamasika austerity. (17.19)

दातव्यमिति यद्दानं दीयतेऽनुपकारिणे ।
देशे काले च पात्रे च तद्दानं सात्त्विकं स्मृतम् ॥१७- २०॥

dAtavyamiti yaddAnaM dIyate.anupakAriNe .
deshe kAle cha pAtre cha taddAnaM sAttvikaM smR^itam.h .. 17\-20..

daatavyaM = worth giving; iti = thus; yat.h = that which; daanaM = charity; diiyate = is given; anupakaariNe = irrespective of return; deshe = in a proper place; kaale = at a proper time; cha = also; paatre = to a suitable person; cha = and; tat.h = that; daanaM = charity; saattvikaM = in the mode of goodness; smR^itaM = is considered.

Charity that is given as a matter of duty, to a deserving candidate who does nothing in return, at the right place and time, is called a Saattvika charity. (17.20)

यत्तु प्रत्युपकारार्थं फलमुद्दिश्य वा पुनः ।
दीयते च परिक्लिष्टं तद्दानं राजसं स्मृतम् ॥१७- २१॥

yattu pratyupakArArthaM phalamuddishya vA punaH .
dIyate cha parikliShTa.n taddAnaM rAjasaM smR^itam.h .. 17\-21..

yat.h = that which; tu = but; pratyupakaaraarthaM = for the sake of getting some return; phalaM = a result; uddishya = desiring; vaa = or; punaH = again; diiyate = is given; cha = also; pariklishhTaM =

grudgingly; tat.h = that; daanaM = charity; raajasaM = in the mode of passion; smR^itaM = is understood to be.

Charity that is given unwillingly, or to get something in return, or looking for some fruit, is called Raajasika charity. (17.21)

अदेशकाले यद्दानमपात्रेभ्यश्च दीयते |
असत्कृतमवज्ञातं तत्तामसमुदाहृतम् ||१७- २२||
adeshakAle yaddAnamapAtrebhyashcha dIyate .
asatkR^itamavaGYAtaM tattAmasamudAhR^itam.h .. 17\-22..

adesha = at an unpurified place; kaale = and unpurified time; yat.h = that which; daanaM = charity; apaatrebhyaH = to unworthy persons; cha = also; diiyate = is given; asatkR^itaM = without respect; avaGYaataM = without proper attention; tat.h = that; taamasaM = in the mode of darkness; udaahR^itaM = is said to be.

Charity that is given at a wrong place and time, to unworthy persons, without paying respect or with contempt, is said to be Taamasika charity. (17.22)

ॐतत्सदिति निर्देशो ब्रह्मणस्त्रिविधः स्मृतः |
ब्राह्मणास्तेन वेदाश्च यज्ञाश्च विहिताः पुरा ||१७- २३||
AUMtatsaditi nirdesho brahmaNastrividhaH smR^itaH .
brAhmaNAstena vedAshcha yaGYAshcha vihitAH purA .. 17\-23..

OM = indication of the Supreme; tat.h = that; sat.h = eternal; iti = thus; nirdeshaH = direction; brahmaNaH = of the Supreme; trividhaH = threefold; smR^itaH = is remembered; braahmaNaaH = the brahmanas (part of Vedic scriptures); tena = with that; vedaaH = the Vedic literature; cha = also; yaGYaaH = sacrifice; cha = also; vihitaaH = used; puraa = formerly.

``OM TAT SAT" is the threefold direction of the Vedic scriptures, The Braahmanas (a class of Vedic scriptures), the Vedas, and the Yajna were ordained from these in the ancient time. (17.23)

तस्मादोमित्युदाहृत्य यज्ञदानतपःक्रियाः |
प्रवर्तन्ते विधानोक्ताः सततं ब्रह्मवादिनाम् ||१७- २४||

tasmAdomityudAhR^itya yaGYadAnatapaHkriyAH .
pravartante vidhAnoktAH satataM brahmavAdinAm.h .. 17\-24..

tasmaat.h = therefore; OM = beginning with om; iti = thus; udaahR^itya = indicating; yaGYa = of sacrifice; daana = charity; tapaH = and penance; kriyaaH = performances; pravartante = begin; vidhaanoktaH = according to scriptural regulation; satataM = always; brahmavaadinaaM = knower of the Supreme.

Therefore, acts of sacrifice, charity, and austerity prescribed in the scriptures are always commenced by uttering ``OM" by the knowers of the Supreme. (17.24)

तदित्यनभिसन्धाय फलं यज्ञतपःक्रियाः |
दानक्रियाश्च विविधाः क्रियन्ते मोक्षकाङ्क्षिभिः ||१७- २५||

tadityanabhisandhAya phalaM yaGYatapaHkriyAH .
dAnakriyAshcha vividhAH kriyante mokShakAN^kShibhiH .. 17\-25..

tat.h = that; iti = thus; anabhisandhaaya = without desiring; phalaM = the fruitive result; yaGYa = of sacrifice; tapaH = and penance; kriyaaH = activities; daana = of charity; kriyaaH = activities; cha = also; vividhaaH = various; kriyante = are done; mokshakaaN^kshibhiH = by those who actually desire liberation.

Various types of sacrifice, charity, and austerity are performed by the seekers of nirvana by uttering ``TAT" (or He is all) without seeking a reward. (17.25)

सद्भावे साधुभावे च सदित्येतत्प्रयुज्यते |
प्रशस्ते कर्मणि तथा सच्छब्दः पार्थ युज्यते ||१७- २६||

sadbhAve sAdhubhAve cha sadityetatprayujyate .
prashaste karmaNi tathA sachchhabdaH pArtha yujyate .. 17\-26..

sad.hbhave = in the sense of the nature of the Supreme, the only reality; saadhubhaave = in the sense of the nature of the devotee; cha = also; sat.h = the word sat; iti = thus; etat.h = this; prayujyate = is used; prashaste = praiseworthy; karmaNi = activities; tathaa = also; sachchhabdaH = the sound sat; paartha = O son of Pritha; yujyate = is used.

SAT is used in the sense of the true reality and goodness. The word ``SAT" is also used for praiseworthy action, O Arjuna. (17.26)

यज्ञे तपसि दाने च स्थितिः सदिति चोच्यते |
कर्म चैव तदर्थीयं सदित्येवाभिधीयते ||१७- २७||
yaGYe tapasi dAne cha sthitiH saditi chochyate .
karma chaiva tadarthIyaM sadityevAbhidhIyate .. 17\-27..

yaGYe = in sacrifice; tapasi = in penance; daane = in charity; cha = also; sthitiH = steadfastness; sat.h = the; Supreme; iti = thus; cha = and; uchyate = is pronounced; karma = work; cha = also; eva = certainly; tat.h = for that; arthiyaM = meant; sat.h = the Supreme; iti = thus; eva = certainly; abhidhiiyate = is indicated.

Steadfastness in sacrifice, charity, and austerity is also called SAT. The action for the sake of the Supreme is verily termed as SAT. (17.27)

अश्रद्धया हुतं दत्तं तपस्तप्तं कृतं च यत् |
असदित्युच्यते पार्थ न च तत्प्रेत्य नो इह ||१७- २८||
ashraddhayA hutaM datta.n tapastapta.n kR^ita.n cha yat.h
.
asadityuchyate pArtha na cha tatpretya no iha .. 17\-28..

ashraddhayaa = without faith; hutaM = offered in sacrifice; dattaM = given; tapaH = penance; taptaM = executed; kR^itaM = performed; cha = also; yat.h = that which; asat.h = false; iti = thus; uchyate = is said to be; paartha = O son of Pritha; na = never; cha = also; tat.h = that; pretya = after death; no = nor; iha = in this life.

Whatever is done without faith; whether it is sacrifice, charity, austerity, or any other act; is called Asat. It has no value here or hereafter, O Arjuna. (17.28)

ॐ तत्सदिति श्रीमद्भगवद्गीतासूपनिषत्सु
ब्रह्मविद्यायां योगशास्त्रे श्रीकृष्णार्जुनसंवादे
श्रद्धात्रयविभागयोगो नाम सप्तदशोऽध्यायः ॥१७॥

AUM tatsaditi shrImadbhagavadgItAsUpaniShatsu
brahmavidyAyA.n yogashAstre
shrIkR^iShNArjunasa.nvAde shraddhAtrayavibhAgayogo
nAma saptadasho.adhyAyaH .. 17

18. Liberation through Renunciation

Introduction:

In the eighteenth discourse, being the last discourse, Lord sums up the whole doctrine of the Gita. It also sums up the entire Vedantic philosophy. The chapter starts with the Arjuna asking about the distinction between Sanyasa and Tyaga. The closest English translation of these words is renunciation and relinquishment, respectively. Explaining the difference between renunciation and relinquishment, Lord says that renouncing is giving up the activities driven by desires, while relinquishing means surrendering the fruits of actions. Although one cannot abandon activities as they are part of the process of living, one must give up the results of her actions, asserts Lord Krishna.

Lord also links the philosophy of Tri-Guna (three attributes theory) to the deeds of an individual and explains how these acts, under the influence of three attributes, bind one to the results if one does not transcend beyond three qualities (Triguna). Lord emphasises not on renouncing actions but giving up deeds with desire.

Key words:

Sanyasa: (सन्यास: itras :sanyAsa) Abondoning desire in work is sanyasa

Tyaga: (त्याग : itrans: tyAga) Relinquishing all fruits of your work is tyaga

Chapter Summary:

The chapter begins with Arjuna expressing his desire to understand the true nature of renunciation (sanyaasa) and relinquishment (tyaga). Replying to the query, Lord Krishna says that the abandonment of desire in actions is *Samyasa* or renunciation. Surrendering the fruits of all deeds is called *Tyaga* or relinquishment.

Divergent views exist among the philosophers about relinquishment. Some sages advise to abandon all actions, whereas the others advocate not to repudiate the acts of sacrifice, charity, and austerity. Concluding that that one must not abandon the acts of charity, austerity and sacrifice, Lord advises to perform them also by leaving aside attachment to fruit. Lord further says that the embodied cannot altogether evade actions, and verily who relinquishes the fruit of action is the real relinquisher. Good, evil, and mixed threefold is the fruit of action for a non-relinquisher, but none for the real relinquisher.

Lord then proceeds to describe this wisdom through the path of Samkhya, where there are five causes to accomplish an action. Samkhya, a system of philosophy based on analysis describes any action as the function of five factors -- the seat of action, the doer, the instruments of action, the various endeavours, and the Supreme.

One with untrained reason sees oneself as the doer, but the one who is free from egoistic notion, even if acting does not see oneself as the doer. The Lord then continues further elaborating the same wisdom through the path of knowledge. He says that if one perceives through the path of knowledge, action has three impulses-- knowledge, acts and the agents.

Viewing through the lens of Samkhya, these three impulses also have three qualities each. That knowledge, by which one sees the one indestructible in all entirety and the undivided Supreme in all separated, is of Satvik quality. Rajasik knowledge perceives several manifold existences in separate entities. By Tamasik understanding a person clings to objects as if they are the whole, the everything, without knowing the reality.

The actions are similarly of three-fold qualities. Those ordained without desire for fruit and attachment, are Satvik actions. Performed with craving, longing for results and with much effort are Rajasik. Executed with delusion without regard to capacity, and consequence, loss and injury to others are Tamasik actions.

Similarly, the performers of actions are also of three qualities. Free from attachment, without ego, endued with firmness and confidence, unchanged with success or failure are of Satvik nature. The agents, who are passionate, wanting the fruit of their actions, and moved with accomplishment or defeat, are of Rajasik nature. Unbalanced, uncultured, stubborn, cheater, malicious, despairing, and procrastinating, such actors are Tamasik.

Lord further says that the division of understanding and determinations is also three-fold. That understanding which knows the distinction between action and non-action, what should be done and what should not be done, what should be the cause of fear and what should not be feared of, what binds and what frees that understanding is satvik.

The reasoning by which one mistakenly understands the difference between right and wrong, and also between effort and lethargy, that reasoning is Rajasik. The reasoning by which one understands wrong as right and interprets all things with their opposite meaning is of Tamasik understanding.

Explaining further the three kinds of determination, Lord says that the unwavering firmness by which, through yoga, one controls the activity of the mind, of the life-breaths and of the sense-organs, that determination is Satvik. The steadfastness by which one holds fast to duty, desire and wealth, that firmness is Rajasik. The determination by which one does not abandon sleep, fear, grief, depression and arrogance, that determination is Tamasik.

After this, Lord proceeds to describe the three kinds of pleasure. Practising this, one rejoices and puts an end to pain. The Satvik pleasure appears as venom in the beginning but as nectar as the outcome. It is born out of the blissful knowledge of the Self. The pleasure derived from the union of the senses with their objects may appear sweet in the beginning. However, its consequences are like poison in the end. That pleasure is Rajasik pleasure. The Tamasik gratification eludes the self, both in the inception and afterwards and arises out of heedlessness, sleep, and indolence. Furthermore, the knowledge of the self eludes Tamsik subjects.

Describing the importance of Guna according to Samkhya philosophy, Lord says that no entity in the entire universe is beyond the control of these three Gunas viz. Satwik, Rajasik, and Tamasik. While dividing the society into four categories, namely Brahmin,

Kshatriya, Vaishya and Shudra, work is assigned to them according to their Gunas arising out of their nature.

For example, attributes such as calmness, self-restraint, austerity, purity and forgiveness, arising out of their nature, the Brahmins are fit to impart wisdom and knowledge and acquire knowledge about the Supreme.

Valour, brilliance, resolution, skill in battle arts, not flying from battle, and generosity, are the attributes suitable for the Kshatriya class engaged in the defence and governing activities.

Farming, rearing animals, and trade are the activities in which Vaishya are involved and are suited to their nature born temperament. Activities and duties of the service class are well suited to the people having inborn qualities of the Shudra class.

Engrossed in their duties emanating from their qualities, a person reaches the abode of the Supreme. He, from whom springs all beings, and who pervades the entire existence, a person attains that Absolute Supreme by worshipping Him in performance of his duties. The Lord further says that it is always better to perform one's duty though destitute of merit, rather than performing the work of others appearing meritorious because the one doing the business laid down by his nature does not incur sin.

One should not abandon the duty assigned as per innate and natural attributes, even if defective, because all the undertakings are clouded by defects, as the fire is clouded by smoke. Whose intelligence is unattached everywhere, who has conquered the ego, and whose desires have gone, who has perfected the art of working with renunciation, he obtains the Supreme.

Attaining Absolute Freedom from Action and State of Brahm:

A person, whose intellect is free from attachment to things and loved ones, who has won oneself, and from whom desires such as for the body, pleasure, power, and objects have gone away, such a person through renunciation achieves the "Naishkarmya Siddhi", the absolute freedom from action. It is a state in which one remains as the actionless Self.

After attaining perfection, how one reaches the state of Absolute (Brahm), that consummation of the knowledge you learn from Me, O Arjuna, says Lord Krishna. A person endowed with pure understanding, resorting to firm self-control, abandoning sound and other objects, casting aside desires and aversions, is fit to become Brahm. Additionally, such a person dwells in solitude, eats less, and has control over speech, body and mind and should constantly meditate, and take refuge in dispassion. Furthermore, a person fit to become Brahm is egoless and peaceful and casts aside egoism, violence, desire, anger and possessions.

Reaching the state of the Brahm, the serene self neither grieves nor desires and considers all being alike and becomes part of the Supreme. He knows Him in essence and becomes one with Him. Such a person though ever performing all worldly actions, by taking the refuge of the Lord, by His grace obtains the timeless, indestructible abode of the Supreme.

The Advice of Lord Krishna to Arjuna:

In the above context, Lord advises Arjuna that he should mentally renounce all work in the Absolute Brahm and take refuge in Buddhi Yoga (the path of unification through wisdom) and thus constantly be aware of the presence of the Supreme.

In such a way, thinking about the Supreme, he will overcome all obstacles by the grace of the Lord (Absolute Brahm). However, if he fails to listen due to egoism, he shall be utterly destroyed. His resolve not to fight under the influence of ego will fail because his warrior nature will contain it. Advising further to Arjuna, Lord says that the deeds due to delusion he wishes not to do, those he shall perform even against his will, fettered by his acts born out of his own nature. The Lord dwells in the hearts of all beings. His illusive power causes all beings to act as though they are mounted on a machine and thus revolving.

Lord says, "go straight to His refuge with your complete being, O Arjun. With His grace, you will find supreme everlasting peace in His abode." Lord further says to Arjuna that the most secret wisdom has been declared to him now, and he may reflect upon it and do whatever he decides.

Uttering the following words to Arjuna, professing the most secret knowledge for his benevolence, Lord further explains -"Merge your mind to Me, be My part, make all efforts for Me, prostrate upon Me, you shall thus come to Me, and I promise that you are the most dear to Me. Do not get confused with the conflicting duties. Surrendering all duties, come to Me for shelter, sorrow not, I will liberate you from all sins.

Cautioning Arjuna, Lord advises not to speak this wisdom to a person who is not willing to listen, and who is without asceticism, devotion, and who speaks evil about the Lord.

"Those who spread this knowledge amongst my devotees are my most beloved devotees themselves", says Krishna. Those who study these dialogues between Lord Krishna and Arjuna, worship Lord through wisdom yoga. The one who listens to these dialogues also get liberated and attains the righteous world.

Lord further asks Arjuna whether his delusion caused by unwisdom has gone away. Arjuna replies that now with the grace of the Lord, his mind is free from confusion, and he is ready to act as advised.

Describing the live conversation between Lord Krishna and Arjuna and hearing the wisdom infused words of the Lord, Sanjay is overwhelmed and rejoices again and again. He further says that where there is Lord Krishna and where there is archer Arjuna, there is prosperity, victory and happiness for sure, that is his opinion.

Analysis::

The Chapter starts with Arjuna's curiousity to understand difference between Sanyasa and Tyaga, which can be loosly transltated as renunciation and relinquishment respectively.

The True Sanyasa:

The Chapter starts with Arjuna's curiosity to understand from the Lord the difference between Sanyasa and Tyaga, Sanskrit words translated loosely as renunciation and relinquishment. Explaining the difference, Lord says-- the word Sanyas comes from Nyas

- the act of giving up. Performing the acts while giving up the desire for the fruit of action is Sanyasa or renunciation. Tyaga, on the other hand, is surrendering or giving up all fruits of their deeds.

Philosophers have been debating about leaving the world in pursuit of everlasting happiness. Many of them advocated abandoning the world to free themselves from the hassles of an active life. Renouncing all worldly affairs, work, and family was commonly known as Sanyasa.

Why did Arjuna ask this question? He could see his friends and relatives on both sides. Bhishma, the grandfather of the dynasty, headed the hostile army of his hundred cousins. Dronacharya, his respected teacher of military tactics, was also among the warriors standing against him in the war.

He was perplexed to see the venerable and the loved ones standing against him on the battlefield, whom he must kill to reclaim his just right. Bewildered by the situation, he was contemplating Sanyasa, where one renounces the world in search of the truth.

According to the doctrine of Karma, actions, whether good or bad, bind a person. Philosophers debate if the actions bind a person, then whether one should relinquish all the acts? Or the acts of Yagya, donation, and austerity should not be given up.

Usually, the people translate Yagya as a Vedic sacrifice, prayer or worship. However, Vedic and Upanishadic literature and chapters 3 and 4 of the Gita hint that Yagya has a broader meaning. To recapitulate, shloka 4.26-28 elaborates:

द्रव्ययज्ञास्तपोयज्ञा योगयज्ञास्तथापरे ।

स्वाध्यायज्ञानयज्ञाश्च यतयः संशितव्रताः ||४- २८||

They offer their wealth, their austerity, and their practice of yoga as an oblation, while the ascetics with strict vows offer their self-study and knowledge as an oblation.

Yagya, therefore, is a selfless act that is performed as an oblation to the Supreme.

Lord Krishna concludes that the acts of Yagya, austerity, and donation are purifiers of intellect and, therefore, should not be relinquished. However, even these acts ought to be performed, giving up attachment and desire for fruits.

Now the question arises if the acts of Yagya, austerity and charity should not be given up, then what about the other actions.

The view of Lord Krishna to renounce actions are not appropriate. Renunciation of action is of three types- Satwik, Rajasik and Tamasik. Giving up the acts because of delusion falls under the category of Tamasik. Relinquishing because of the fear of physical suffering falls under the category of Rajasik relinquishment. Rajasik and Tamasik relinquishments do not result in peace of mind or a blissful experience.

Satwik abandoning is the abandonment of the attachment and the fruit of actions.

Lord further clarifies that in addition to the prescribed acts of austerity, charity and Yagya, one needs to perform several pleasant and unpleasant deeds. Satwik relinquishers neither hate the unpleasant work nor are attached to the pleasant one and can overcome all their doubts. No one can give up all the activities as they are obligatory in the process of living. Therefore, the one who relinquishes the fruit of action, not the deed itself, is the real relinquisher.

Three Kinds of the fruit of action:

Now, after explaining that giving up all action is impossible for the living being, Lord proceeds to elucidate the results of various deeds.

We observe that every action has its consequences. The outcome can be favourable to the person performing that action, or it can be unfavourable. The task can have mixed results where some parts of the consqunces are positive, while the other parts of it are negative.

Have you ever imagined why one classifies those outcomes as favourable, unfavourable or mixed? When you desire some result while performing a task, and that you get, you consider that as a positive outcome. However, when you execute a deed because it is your duty, or you consider it a divine service for the benefit of the environment or society, you are not attached by the outcome. Your mental state is not affected by the consequence of the task performed. Performing an assignment with such an attitude is an attribute of Sanyasis. Lord, therefore, says that avidya-generated actions and the threefold fruit of action - evil, pleasant, and mixed do not accrue to the Sanyasis.

Analysis of the Doership of a Task

To make Arjuna understand the subject in more detail and relinquish the idea of agency in a task, Lord elucidate the analysis of various components in performing an act according to the Samkhya system.

He explains the five causes of accomplishment of all actions -- the physical body, the doer (subject), the instrument, the effort, and a factor of chance.

The role of the physical body, the effort, and the instruments of execution are well comprehendible. Let us understand the other two factors- the chance and the doer. Chance is a factor of uncertainty, common with most human endeavours. Its causes may be past actions, actions of others, and the environment which affects the outcome of an act.

One may be puzzled why Lord has listed the physical body (Adhishthan) and the doer (Karta) separately as causes of the attainment of an action. Are not they the same? The physical body is the instrument by which you execute the work. The doer of the work is you, not your body. According to Samkhya philosophy, Purush and Prakriti together make your pseudo-self (ego), which thinks of itself as the real doer. Purusha (True Self) is merely a witness in all actions.

Whatever action, whether just or unjust, one performs using his body, mind, or speech, the above five are their causes.

Delusion causes people to believe that they are the real doer. However, those who are free from the idea of the agency may kill from the worldly point of view, but they slay not and remain unbound from the results of their actions. Here Lord does not give us immunity to commit crimes. The one whose consciousness is united in the universal spirit does not need to commit offences.

Evil activities spring from ignorance about the true nature of the Self. Here the Lord sums up the teachings introduced in previous discourses where he declares that the true nature of the Self is immutable and the Self remains a spectator only and does not act. Shankaracharya explains in his commentary that in the absence of an egoistic feeling of embodied existence, the Sanyasis renounce the idea of agency while doing a task.

Mental Incitement and Execution of an Action

Further analysis of actions reveals that they require mental incitement and physical execution. Three essential elements to mentally incite an action are -- knowledge, the object of knowledge and the knower. They together form a group of threefold incitement of action.

After mental incitement, the physical execution of work requires at least an actor, an instrument and the action. They together make a group of the threefold basis of action.

Take a simple task to understand it more lucidly. For example, if you are planning to plant a tree. The idea of planting a tree and its planning involves knowledge of trees, their planting and various steps involved in the process. We, therefore, see that this simple mental incitement requires three essential elements of mental provocation-- you, your knowledge and your object of knowledge (the process of tree plantation).

The physical execution of the plan also requires three essential elements- the actor (you), the act (of plantation) and the instrument (your hands or any other tool). Here the actor is not your true Self but the ego. True Self remains as the spectator and does not act.

The knowledge, the actor and the deeds are part of the manifested nature and are, therefore, of three types—Satwik, Rajasik, and Tamasik like all other expressions of nature.

Classification of Knowledge, Deed and the Doer:

After explaining the mechanism of action, Lord proceeds to describe the three categories of knowledge, deed, and the doer based on the Samkhya doctrine.

Etymologically, Samkhya in Sanskrit is from numbers, analysis or reasoning. Pratyaksh (direct sensory perception), Anuman (inference), and Shabd (Word or reliable source) are the three valid means of knowledge according to the Samkhya doctrine. The great philosopher Maharshi Kapil, a Vedik Rishi, is considered the original proponent of Samkhya philosophy. Kapil Rishi was one of the most revered scholars of ancient India who also influenced Buddhism and Jainism.

According to Samkhya, the world is composed of Purusha and Prakriti. Purusha is the witness, consciousness and observer and is the same as the Brahm or the Self of the Upnishads. Prakriti, that originates the matter in the universe is the unconscious part of it. It consists of three characteristics - Sattvik, Rajasik and Tamasik.

Sattvik Guna refers to poise, elegance, luminance and bliss. Rajasik refers to vigour, activity, excitation and pain, and Tamas is similar to inertia, grossness, heaviness, laziness and obstruction.

Unmanifested Prakriti is in a state of equilibrium and is endless and beginningless like the conciousness. When it comes into contact with Purusha, it gives rise to the manifested world of experience.

More about Three Gunas:

As explained in chapter 13, shloka 19 & 21, Lord has described both Purusha and Prakriti as endless and beginningless. Purusha seated in Prakriti enjoys the Gunas created by Prakriti. Attachment to the Gunas is the cause of birth and re-birth in various wombs.

The "Three-Guna" concept originated in Samkhya philosophy and found its way into most Indian schools of philosophy. The three Gunas originating from Prakriti are Satwik, Rajasik and Tamasik. The three Gunas constantly interact in a playful illusionary state called Maya. The pattern of the interplay of Gunas varying in relative amounts defines the essential qualities of someone or something. We humans can consciously alter the relative amount of various Gunas in ourselves using our willpower, thoughts and lifestyle.

Three Gunas and their attributes:

Tamasik guna is associated with lethargy, darkness, ignorance, shame, guilt, depression, addiction, apathy, confusion, grief etc. Tamasik Guna binds one by ignorance and inertia.

Rajasik Guna corresponds to energy, movement, and action. Other rajasic qualities are attachment, anger, passion, worry, fear, restlessness, and anxiety. Rajasik Guna strongly binds one to the fruit of her action. Rajasik Guna binds one through passion and craving.

Satwik Guna is associated with harmony, balance, joy, and intelligence. Other Satwik qualities are happiness, peace, love, compassion, equanimity, focus, self-control, and trust. Satwik Guna binds through attachment to knowledge and joy.

While rajasic and tamasic Gunas create the immediate downfall of a person by binding her to the fruit of her action, Satwik Guna, although binding initially, can provide her with the path to ultimate freedom by making one fit to go beyond the Three Gunas.

Therefore, all the three Gunas bind the embodied through attachment. To attain freedom, one needs to transcend these three Gunas.

Classification of Knowledge:

Based on the above classification, Satvik knowledge is the one by which one indestructible Supreme, the Purusha of the Samkhya, is seen inseparable in all separate entities.

But the knowledge which considers several septate existences of all beings is Rajasik knowledge.

Tamasik knowledge is engrossed in one single effect, is narrow, thinking that it is the whole, without reason, and without understanding the reality. For example, due to Tamasik knowledge, people believe that this body is everything, and they spend their whole life fulfilling the needs of their bodies like hunger and lust. Some of the beliefs not founded on reason, for example-- a temple or the Kaaba is the house of God, originate from Tamasik knowledge of the people having no discriminating knowledge.

Classification of Action:

Now Lord proceeds to explain the classification of action based on Samkhya philosophy.

Ordained actions, undesirous of fruit, devoid of attachment, without love or hate, are classified as Satvik.

The obligatory duties, which no one can escape, are of two kinds. The routine deeds, that one needs to perform as a process of living falls under one category. The other category consists of assignments that a person must do in the social hierarchy or employment. Satvik actions are obligatory duties devoid of attachment to the fruit of action and free from any feeling of love or hate towards those actions.

Sometimes, one performs some actions to achieve desired objectives, under the influence of ego, thinking that he is fit to achieve what he wants. The desire may originate from seeing others or assuming the aim wrongly within own capabilities. In such cases, such actions may require tremendous effort and can cause anxiety.

The undertakings to fulfil ambitions, where one works hard to achieve those endeavours and constantly feels the pinch of extreme efforts, are a sign of Rajasik actions. The actions performed with great strain, with ego, and longing for desire are called Rajasik actions.

The consequences of which are loss, injury to oneself or others, undertaken without assessing capabilities and outcomes are called Tamasic.

Classification of Doers:

After explaining the classification of actions, Lord proceeds to explain the categories of agents as follows. Liberated from attachment, free of ego, endued with firmness and vigour, unaffected in success and failure, these are the qualities of the Satvik agent.

Passionate, wanting to obtain the fruit of action, greedy, impure, cruel, and the one who is moved easily by joy or sorrow is called Rajasik doer.

We encounter people who have a great attachment to some cause, person, position, goal or ambition. They desire to attain their dream at any cost. They always act to obtain a reward for their actions. They are greedy as they want to possess the worldly things they desire. Their heart is not pure, as they can deceit or adopt evil means to attain their goals. Their deep attachment to the object of affection makes them prone to strong emotions of joy and sorrow on achieving success or failure.

The doer who is unbalanced, uncultured, obstinate, cheater, malicious, lazy, despairing, and procrastinating, such a doer is called Tamasik.

Who is the actor here? Lord has described the doers in three categories here, but in verse sixteen, he says that the person with an untrained intellect assumes his Self to be the actor. The ego, therefore, is the actor that considers itself to be the actor. In the absence of ego, the person is not bound by the actions performed.

Three Types of Intellect and Resolve:

Lord further elaborates that division of intellect and resolve is also of three types according to qualities.

The understanding by which one can discriminate between action and non-action, what ought to be done and what not ought to be done, fear and fearlessness, and bondage and liberation that intellect is Satwik.

The understanding by which one wrongly discriminates between Dharma (right) and Adharma (wrong), what ought to be done and what not ought to be done, that intellect is Rajasik.

Intellect shrouded in the darkness, thinking wrong as right and right as wrong and seeing all things opposite of what they are, that intellect is Tamasik.

Similarly, the resolve is also of three types-Satvik, Rajasik and Tamasik.

Achieved through yoga, the unflinching firmness that restrains the activities of the mind, breath, and sense organs is called Satvik.

The firmness through which one holds fast the Dharma(duty) pleasure and wealth desirous of fruit is Rajasik.

One may understand the importance of duty, money and desires for an ideal life. Scriptures extoll duty, money, sexual desire, and liberation as the four aims of life. However, these aims also should not be pursued with the desire for fruit to classify under the Satwik category.

Due to the lack of firmness, if one does not give up sleep, fear, grief, depression, and lust, that resolve is Tamasik.

Three Kinds of Pleasure:

Further elaborating on the classification of pleasure, Lord says that happiness is also of three kinds- Satwik, Rajasik and Tamasik. The delight which initially appears as venom but finally as nectar that pleasure is called Satwik and is born out of blissful knowledge of the Self.

The happiness resulting from the union of senses with their objects may initially appear like nectar, but in the end like poison, is Rajasik. That delight which deludes the subject at the beginning and the end, and which arises from sleep, sloth and delinquency is called Tamasik pleasure.

No physical entity can be without the three attributes of Satvik, Rajasik and Tamasik qualities associated with nature.

Division of Society in Four Classes:

A society needs some products and services to survive, flourish and achieve self-actualization.

Vedic philosophers identified the basic services as -

- knowledge work and education
- defence, administration and governing of the state
- agriculture, animal husbandry, and trade.
- Other services.

The division of society into four classes is called the Varna system. Varna in Sanskrit means colour. It is interesting to know why scriptures named the division of society Chatur Varna- a system of four colours.

Colours represent classification based on a nominal scale as no colour is inferior to another. Had it been named after alphabets or numerals, people would confuse it with an ordinal scale, indicating the one appearing in the beginning as the superior.

All Varnas are equal is also evident from the fact that in Purush Sukta of the Rig Veda where the Varna system finds its first mention, compares the four Varnas with four vital organs of Purusha (literally a man).

Contrary to popular perceptions, and later distortions, according to the ancient texts, the Varna system was not heredity based. Lord explicitly mentions that the formation of four classes is based on attributes and actions, not on birth.

In chapter four of shloka 13 Lord says:

चातुर्वर्ण्यं मया सृष्टं गुणकर्मविभागशः ।

I (The Lord) created the four Varna based on the division of attributes and actions of individuals.

Here in Shloka 41 of chapter 18, Lord reiterates - Of Brahmin, Kshatriya, Vaishya and Shudra, duties have been assigned based on their nature-produced qualities.

Attributes born out of their nature, which make them suitable for the duties of Brahmin are - calmness, self-control, austerity, purity, forgiveness and also uprightness, wisdom, knowledge and belief in God.

Similarly, some people are suitable for the duties of Kshatriya, having inborn qualities such as prowess, splendour firmness, dexterity, not flying away from the battlefield, generosity etc. These qualities are most suitable for warriors, kings and rulers.

Further, agriculture, protection of kine, and trade are the duties assigned to Vaishya based on their inborn nature. Service to all the three classes of society is most suitable for people who are happy to follow instructions and have no aptitude to learn the skills of the other three classes.

An important point to note here is that in these verses, Lord has emphasised that the division of classes is based on nature-born attributes. Nowhere he has mentioned the basis of division as ancestry.

Division of work based on natural inclination, attributes and skills has considerable advantages over societies where heredity or reward dictates the choice of duties. The biggest is the intrinsic pleasure that one obtains while performing the tasks.

Engrossed in the duty assigned according to their nature, people accomplish perfection. Enjoying their work, they achieve the bliss of uniting with the Supreme. Lord further elaborates that doing the job according to one's nature with complete involvement is like worshipping that Supreme who has created all the beings and by which this whole universe is pervaded.

The phenomenon Lord Krishna is talking about in these verses is often called the flow state by modern psychologists. In the flow state, one experiences a fluidity between her body and mind, totally immersed and deeply engrossed in something beyond the point of distraction. The distinguishing factors of the flow state are-

1. Focused attention on the present moment.
2. Merging of action and awareness

3. Loss of reflective cognition.
4. Altered time consciousness
5. Perceiving the activity as intrinsically rewarding without caring about the outcome.

Lord further says that innate endeavours, even if perceived defective, should not be abandoned. Only nature-born work has the potential to induce optimal experience. Defects in work are inevitable, just like the smoke clouding the fire is imminent.

Karm Yoga and Absolute Perfection:

He, whose understanding is unattached everywhere, who has won himself and whose desires have gone, attains the supreme state of freedom from action through renunciation.

A person who is not attached to his possessions, his dear ones like wife and children, and whose mind is not disturbed with ever unsatiable desires for the body, life and pleasure, is fit for attaining Neshkramya Siddhi. Neshkramya Siddhi is the state of perfection leading to freedom from action, where the activities do not bind an individual to their outcome.

Additionally, Brahm does not act, but the nature by the power of the Supreme is the cause of all actions. Reaching the state of the Supreme is the perfect state where one becomes actionless and attains Neshkarmya Siddhi. As Brahm is the source of all understanding and knowledge, gaining his state, one achieves the highest wisdom that Lord Krishna proceeds to describe succinctly.

The one who attains the state of the Brahm has access to pure wisdom. As a result, he can control the

Self with firmness, having abandoned sound and other objects, and laying aside passion and hatred. He dwells in solitude, eats less, has subdued speech, body, and mind and always engages in meditation.

Additionally, such a person would relinquish egoism, strength, arrogance, desire, malice, and property, and is free from the concept of mine and is always peaceful. Attaining the state of Brahm, he reaches the abode of the Supreme and becomes part of Him.

Becoming part of the Lord, he knows Him in essence, and thus essentially enters into Him.

Art of Action to attain the Supreme:

Lord further elaborates how one can reach Him while performing worldly actions. He says, while doing all actions whatsoever, taking refuge in Him, one reaches the abode of the supreme, by the grace of the Lord. One should mentally surrender all work to the Supreme, and using mental concentration, should fix her heart to the Supreme. By fixing her heart on the supreme, one crosses all difficulties easily, but if due to ego, the one who doesn't understand will perish.

Lord further says to Arjuna that if thinking of himself as an intelligent and knowledgable person due to ego, he decides not to fight, his Kshatriya nature will compel him still to fight the war. Lord further elaborates that like everyone, Arjuna is bound by his duty as a warrior, which is born out of his nature, and will coerce him to fight against his own will.

Furthermore, Lord says that The Supreme sits in the heart of everyone, and the creatures move and act under the influence of Maya created by God like a doll mounted on a machine. Lord advises Arjuna to go to His refuge with all his being to obtain peace in the eternal resting place. Saying this Lord enunciates that the most secret wisdom has been revealed to Arjuna, and he should reflect on it and act as he desires.

Further, Lord reveals even more secret wisdom for the benefit of Arjuna and the man-kind. He advises Arjuna to merge his mind with Lord, to become His part, to work by surrendering the fruit of action to the Lord, thus he will surely come to the abode of the Lord. Further, Lord says, abandoning all confusion about right and wrong deeds, take refuge in Him and He will liberate Arjuna from all sins, therefore he should not grieve.

Lord advises Arjuna not to reveal this secret knowledge to someone who is not ascetic or devoted and also not to the one who is not interested to listen or the one who speaks evil about the Lord. He further says, however the one who shares this knowledge with the people who have faith on the Lord and devoted to Him, does the greates service to the Lord. Even the study of this secret dialogue is like the worship of the Supreme with Wisdom Yoga. Further, the person who listens this secret dialogue also gets the benefits and attains the abode of the Supreme.

Lord then asks Arjuna, whether his unwisdom has gone or still persisiting.Arjuna replies that with the grace of the Lord his delusion has disappreared and now he will do according to the words of the Lord.

Sanjay, describing the situation from the war field to Dritrashtra says, listning to these dialogues between

Lord and Arjuna, he rejoices again and again. Wherever there is Lord Krishna the Lord of Yoga and wherever there is archer the Arjuna, victory , prosperity and happiness is assured this is my opinion.

Original Sanskrit with Word Meanings, Transliteration and Translation (Chapter-18)

अथाष्टादशोऽध्यायः । मोक्षसंन्यासयोगः

atha AShTAdasho.adhyAyaH .
mokShasa.nnyAsayogaH
Here begins the eighteenth chapter
(mokShasa.nnyAsayogaH)

अर्जुन उवाच ।
संन्यासस्य महाबाहो तत्त्वमिच्छामि वेदितुम् ।
त्यागस्य च हृषीकेश पृथक्केशिनिषूदन ॥१८- १॥

sa.nnyAsasya mahAbAho tattvamichchhAmi veditum.h .
tyAgasya cha hR^iShIkesha pR^ithakkeshiniShUdana .. 18\-1..

arjuna uvaacha = Arjuna said; sa.nnyaasasya = of renunciation; mahaabaaho = O mighty-armed one; tattvaM = the essence; ichchhaami = I wish; vedituM = to understand; tyaagasya = of abandonment; cha = also; hR^ishhiikesha = O; master of the senses; pR^ithak.h = severally; keshinishuudana = O killer of the Keshi demon.

Arjuna said: I wish to know severally the essenece of renunciation O Hrishikesha (Krishna) and of relinquishment, O Slayer of Demon Keshi (Lord Krishna). (18.01)

श्रीभगवानुवाच ।
काम्यानां कर्मणां न्यासं संन्यासं कवयो विदुः ।
सर्वकर्मफलत्यागं प्राहुस्त्यागं विचक्षणाः ॥१८- २॥

shrIbhagavAnuvAcha .
kAmyAnA.n karmaNA.n nyAsaM sa.nnyAsaM kavayo viduH .
sarvakarmaphalatyAgaM prAhustyAgaM vichakShaNAH .. 18\-2..

shriibhagavaanuvaacha = the Supreme Lord said; kaamyaanaaM = with desire; karmaNaaM = of activities; nyaasaM = renouncing; sa.nnyaasaM = renounciation; kavayaH = the learned; viduH = know;

sarva = of all; karma = activities; phala = of results; tyaagaM = relinquishment; praahuH = call; tyaagaM = renunciation; vichakshaNaH = the experienced.

The Supreme Lord said: The sages call renunciation the abondonment of selfish work. Relinquishing the fruit of all actions is called the relinquishment by the wise. (18.02)

त्याज्यं दोषवदित्येके कर्म प्राहुर्मनीषिणः।
यज्ञदानतपःकर्म न त्याज्यमिति चापरे ॥१८- ३॥
tyAjya.n doShavadityeke karma prAhurmanIShiNaH .
yaGYadAnatapaHkarma na tyAjyamiti chApare .. 18\-3..

tyaajyaM = must be given up; doshhavat.h = as an evil; iti = thus; eke = one group; karma = work; praahuH = they say; maniishhiNaH = great thinkers; yaGYa = of sacrifice; daana = charity; tapaH = and penance; karma = works; na = never; tyaajyaM = are to be given up; iti = thus; cha = and; apare = others.

Actions should be relinquished as an evil, declare some thoughtful man, still the others have the view that sacrifice, charity and austerity should not be relinquished. (18.03)

निश्चयं शृणु मे तत्र त्यागे भरतसत्तम।
त्यागो हि पुरुषव्याघ्र त्रिविधः सम्प्रकीर्तितः ॥१८- ४॥
nishchayaM shR^iNu me tatra tyAge bharatasattama .
tyAgo hi puruShavyAghra trividhaH samprakIrtitaH .. 18\-4..

nishchayaM = certainty; shR^iNu = hear; me = from Me; tatra = therein; tyaage = in the matter of renunciation; bharatasattama = O best of the Bharatas; tyaagaH = renunciation; hi = certainly; purushhavyaaghra = O tiger among human beings; trividhaH = of three kinds; samprakiirtitaH = is declared.

Listen to My conclusion about relinquishment. It is said to be of three types, O tiger amongst the men. (18.04)

यज्ञदानतपःकर्म न त्याज्यं कार्यमेव तत्।
यज्ञो दानं तपश्चैव पावनानि मनीषिणाम् ॥१८- ५॥
yaGYadAnatapaHkarma na tyAjya.n kAryameva tat.h .
yaGYo dAnaM tapashchaiva pAvanAni manIShiNAm.h .. 18\-5..

yaGYa = of sacrifice; daana = charity; tapaH = and penance; karma = activity; na = never; tyaajyaM = to be given up; kaaryaM = must be done; eva = certainly; tat.h = that; yaGYaH = sacrifice; daanaM = charity; tapaH = penance; cha = also; eva = certainly; paavanaani = purifying; maniishhiNaaM = even for the great souls.

Acts of sacrifice, charity, and austerity should not be abandoned, but should be performed, because sacrifice, charity, and austerity are the purifiers of the wise. (18.05)

एतान्यपि तु कर्माणि सङ्गं त्यक्त्वा फलानि च ।
कर्तव्यानीति मे पार्थ निश्चितं मतमुत्तमम् ॥१८- ६॥

etAnyapi tu karmANi saN^ga.n tyaktvA phalAni cha .
kartavyAnIti me pArtha nishchitaM matamuttamam.h .. 18\-6..

etaani = all these; api = certainly; tu = but; karmaaNi = activities; saN^gaM = association; tyaktvaa = renouncing; phalaani = results; cha = also; kartavyaani = should be done as duty; iti = thus; me = My; paartha = O son of Pritha; nishchitaM = definite; mataM = opinion; uttamaM = the best.

Even these (obligatory) works should be performed without attachment to the fruits as a duty. This is My definite supreme advice, O Arjuna. (18.06)

नियतस्य तु संन्यासः कर्मणो नोपपद्यते ।
मोहात्तस्य परित्यागस्तामसः परिकीर्तितः ॥१८- ७॥

niyatasya tu sa.nnyAsaH karmaNo nopapadyate .
mohAttasya parityAgastAmasaH pariklrtitaH .. 18\-7..

niyatasya = prescribed; tu = but; sa.nnyaasaH = renunciation; karmaNaH = of activities; na = never; upapadyate = is deserved; mohaat.h = by illusion; tasya = of them; parityaagaH = renunciation; taamasaH = in the mode of ignorance; parikiirtitaH = is declared.

Verily renunciation of actions that are prescribed is not proper ; the relinquishment thereof from delusion is said to be tamasik. (18.07)

दुःखमित्येव यत्कर्म कायक्लेशभयात्त्यजेत् ।
स कृत्वा राजसं त्यागं नैव त्यागफलं लभेत् ॥१८- ८॥

duHkhamityeva yatkarma kAyakleshabhayAttyajet.h .

sa kR^itvA rAjasaM tyAgaM naiva tyAgaphalaM labhet.h .. 18\-8..

duHkhaM = unhappy; iti = thus; eva = certainly; yat.h = which; karma = work; kaaya = for the body; klesha = trouble; bhayaat.h = out of fear; tyajet.h = gives up; saH = he; kR^itvaa = after doing; raajasaM = in the mode of passion; tyaagaM = renunciation; na = not; eva = certainly; tyaaga = of renunciation; phalaM = the results; labhet.h = gains.

One who abandons actions from the fear of physical sufferings, does not get the benefits of relinquishment by performing such Raajasika relinquishment. (18.08)

कार्यमित्येव यत्कर्म नियतं क्रियतेऽर्जुन ।
सङ्गं त्यक्त्वा फलं चैव स त्यागः सात्त्विको मतः ॥१८- ९॥
kAryamityeva yatkarma niyataM kriyate.arjuna .
saN^ga.n tyaktvA phala.n chaiva sa tyAgaH sAttviko mataH .. 18\-9..

kaaryaM = it must be done; iti = thus; eva = indeed; yat.h = which; karma = work; niyataM = prescribed; kriyate = is performed; arjuna = O Arjuna; saN^gaM = association; tyaktvaa = giving up; phalaM = the result; cha = also; eva = certainly; saH = that; tyaagaH = renunciation; saattvikaH = in the mode of goodness; mataH = in My opinion.

Obligatory work performed as duty because it ought to be done, renouncing attachment and also the fruit, is alone regarded as Saattvika relinquishment, O Arjuna. (18.09)

न द्वेष्ट्यकुशलं कर्म कुशले नानुषज्जते ।
त्यागी सत्त्वसमाविष्टो मेधावी छिन्नसंशयः ॥१८- १०॥
na dveShTyakushalaM karma kushale nAnuShajjate .
tyAgI sattvasamAviShTo medhAvI chhinnasa.nshayaH .. 18\-10..

na = never; dveshhTi = hates; akushalaM = inauspicious; karma = work; kushale = in the auspicious; na = nor

anushhajjate = becomes attached; tyaagii = the renouncer; sattva = in goodness; samaavishhTaH = absorbed; medhaavii = intelligent; chhinna = having cut off; sa.nshayaH = all doubts.

One who neither hates an evil work nor is attached to an agreeable work, is renunciate, Saattvika, wise and cuts usunder all doubts. (18.10)

न हि देहभृता शक्यं त्यक्तुं कर्माण्यशेषतः ।
यस्तु कर्मफलत्यागी स त्यागीत्यभिधीयते ॥१८- ११॥
na hi dehabhR^itA shakya.n tyaktuM karmANyasheShataH
.
yastu karmaphalatyAgI sa tyAgItyabhidhIyate .. 18\-11..

na = never; hi = certainly; dehabhR^itaa = by the embodied; shakyaM = is possible; tyaktuM = to be renounced; karmaaNi = activities; asheshhataH = altogether; yaH = anyone who; tu = but; karma = of work; phala = of the result; tyaagii = the renouncer; saH = he; tyaagii = the renouncer; iti = thus; abhidhiiyate = is said.

Nor indeed it is possible to relinquish actions completely; the one who relinquishes the fruit of action is real relinquisher. (18.11)

अनिष्टमिष्टं मिश्रं च त्रिविधं कर्मणः फलम् ।
भवत्यत्यागिनां प्रेत्य न तु संन्यासिनां क्वचित् ॥१८- १२॥
aniShTamiShTaM mishra.n cha trividhaM karmaNaH phalam.h .
bhavatyatyAginAM pretya na tu sa.nnyAsinA.n kvachit.h .. 18\-12..

anishhTaM = leading to hell; ishhTaM = leading to heaven; mishraM = mixed; cha = and; trividhaM = of three kinds; karmaN;aH = of work; phalaM = the result; bhavati = comes; atyaaginaaM = for those who are not renounced; pretya = after death; na = not; tu = but; sa.nnyaasiinaaM = for the renounced order; kvachit.h = at any time.

Good, evil and mixed threefold is the fruit of action hereafter for the non- relinquisher; but none ever for the relinquisher. (18.12)

पञ्चैतानि महाबाहो कारणानि निबोध मे ।
साङ्ख्ये कृतान्ते प्रोक्तानि सिद्धये सर्वकर्मणाम् ॥१८- १३॥
pa~nchaitAni mahAbAho kAraNAni nibodha me .
sAN^khye kR^itAnte proktAni siddhaye sarvakarmaNAm.h .. 18\-13..

paJNcha = five; etaani = these; mahaabaaho = O mighty-armed one; kaaraNaani = causes; nibodha = just; understand; me = from Me; saaN^khye = in the Vedanta; kR^itaante = in the conclusion; proktaani = said; siddhaye = for the perfection; sarva = of all; karmaNaaM = activities.

Five are the causes, O mighty armed (Arjuna), understand from Me; that have been declared according to Samkhya said to be essential for perfection in all action. (18.13)

अधिष्ठानं तथा कर्ता करणं च पृथग्विधम् ।
विविधाश्च पृथक्चेष्टा दैवं चैवात्र पञ्चमम् ॥१८- १४॥
adhiShThAnaM tathA kartA karaNa.n cha pR^ithagvidham.h .
vividhAshcha pR^ithakcheShTA daiva.n chaivAtra pa~nchamam.h .. 18\-14..

adhishhThaanaM = the place; tathaa = also; kartaa = the worker; karaNaM = instruments; cha = and; pR^ithag.hvidhaM = of different kinds; vividhaH = various; cha = and; pR^ithak.h = separate; cheshhTaH = the endeavors; daivaM = the divinity or the Supreme; cha = also; eva = certainly; atra = here; paJNchamaM = the fifth.

The place, the doer, and the instruments or organs of various sorts; the various endeavours and the divinity the fifth one.(18.14)

शरीरवाङ्मनोभिर्यत्कर्म प्रारभते नरः ।
न्याय्यं वा विपरीतं वा पञ्चैते तस्य हेतवः ॥१८- १५॥
sharIravAN^manobhiryatkarma prArabhate naraH .
nyAyya.n vA viparItaM vA pa~nchaite tasya hetavaH .. 18\-15..

shariira = by the body; vaak.h = speech; manobhiH = and mind; yat.h = which; karma = work; praarabhate = begins; naraH = a person; nyaayyaM = right; vaa = or; vipariitaM = the opposite; vaa = or; paJNcha = five; ete = all these; tasya = its; hetavaH = causes.

Whatever action, whether right or the opposite, one performs by deed, word, and thought; these five are the causes thereof. (18.15)

तत्रैवं सति कर्तारमात्मानं केवलं तु यः ।

पश्यत्यकृतबुद्धित्वान्न स पश्यति दुर्मतिः ||१८- १६||

tatraivaM sati kartAramAtmAnaM kevalaM tu yaH .
pashyatyakR^itabuddhitvAnna sa pashyati durmatiH .. 18\-16..

tatra = there; evaM = thus; sati = being; kartaaraM = the doer; aatmaanaM = himself; kevalaM = only; tu = but; yaH = anyone who; pashyati = sees; akR^itabuddhitvaat.h = due to unintelligence; na = never; saH = he; pashyati = sees; durmatiH = foolish.

This being the case; the ignorant person who considers oneself as the sole agent due to imperfect understanding does not understand.(18.16)

यस्य नाहंकृतो भावो बुद्धिर्यस्य न लिप्यते |
हत्वाऽपि स इमाँल्लोकान्न हन्ति न निबध्यते ||१८- १७||

yasya nAha.nkR^ito bhAvo buddhiryasya na lipyate .
hatvA.api sa imA.NllokAnna hanti na nibadhyate .. 18\-17..

yasya = one whose; na = never; ahaN^kR^itaH = of false ego; bhaavaH = nature; buddhiH = intelligence; yasya = one whose; na = never; lipyate = is attached; hatvaa = killing; api = even; saH = he; imaan.h = this; lokaan.h = world; na = never; hanti = kills; na = never; nibadhyate = becomes entangled.

The one who is free from the notion of doership and whose wisdom is not attached; even after slaying these people, neither slays nor is bound (by the act of killing). (18.17)

ज्ञानं ज्ञेयं परिज्ञाता त्रिविधा कर्मचोदना |
करणं कर्म कर्तेति त्रिविधः कर्मसंग्रहः ||१८- १८||

GYAnaM GYeyaM pariGYAtA trividhA karmachodanA .
karaNaM karma karteti trividhaH karmasa.ngrahaH .. 18\-18..

GYaanaM = knowledge; GYeyaM = the objective of knowledge; pariGYaataa = the knower; trividhaa = of three kinds; karma = of work; chodanaa = the impetus; karaNaM = the senses; karma = the work; kartaa = the doer; iti = thus; trividhaH = of three kinds; karma = of work; sa.ngrahaH = the accumulation.

The knowledge, the knowable (object of knowledge) and the knower, these three are the impetus of action; the

instruments of action (organs), the action and the agent (doer) are the three fold basis of the action.(18.18)

ज्ञानं कर्म च कर्ताच त्रिधैव गुणभेदतः ।
प्रोच्यते गुणसङ्ख्याने यथावच्छृणु तान्यपि ॥१८- १९॥

GYAnaM karma cha kartAcha tridhaiva guNabhedataH .
prochyate guNasaN^khyAne yathAvachchhR^iNu tAnyapi .. 18\-19..

GYaanaM = knowledge; karma = work; cha = also; kartaa = worker; cha = also; tridhaa = of three kinds; eva = certainly; guNabhedataH = based on the Guna or natural atrributes; prochyate = are said; guNasa.nkhyaane = according to Samkhya doctrine of Guna or attributes; yathaavat.h = as they are; shR^iNu = hear; taani = all of them; api = also.

The knowledge), the action, and the agent are said to be of three types according to the Guna theory of Saamkhya doctrine. Hear duly about these also. (18.19)

सर्वभूतेषु येनैकं भावमव्ययमीक्षते ।
अविभक्तं विभक्तेषु तज्ज्ञानं विद्धि सात्त्विकम् ॥१८- २०॥

sarvabhUteShu yenaikaM bhAvamavyayamIkShate .
avibhakta.n vibhakteShu tajGYAnaM viddhi sAttvikam.h .. 18\-20..

sarvabhuuteshhu = in all living entities; yena = by which; ekaM = one; bhaavaM = situation; avyayaM = imperishable; iikshate = one sees; avibhaktaM = undivided; vibhakteshhu = in the divided; tat.h = that; GYaanaM = knowledge; viddhi = know; saattvikaM = in the mode of goodness.

Knowledge by which one sees a single imperishable reality in all beings as undivided in the divided; such knowledge is considered to be Saattvika. (18.20)

पृथक्त्वेन तु यज्ज्ञानं नानाभावान्पृथग्विधान् ।
वेत्ति सर्वेषु भूतेषु तज्ज्ञानं विद्धि राजसम् ॥१८- २१॥

pR^ithaktvena tu yajGYAnaM nAnAbhAvAnpR^ithagvidhAn.h .

vetti sarveShu bhUteShu tajGYAnaM viddhi rAjasam.h .. 18\-21..

pR^ithaktvena = because of division; tu = but; yat.h = which; GYaanaM = knowledge; naanaabhaavaan.h = multifarious situations; pR^ithag.hvidhaan.h = different; vetti = knows; sarveshhu = in all; bhuuteshhu = living entities; tat.h = that; GYaanaM = knowledge; viddhi = must be known; raajasaM = in terms of passion.

Knowledge which regards several manifoeld existences in all beings as separate from one another, know that knowledge to be Raajasika. (18.21)

यत्तु कृत्स्नवदेकस्मिन्कार्ये सक्तमहैतुकम् ।
अतत्त्वार्थवदल्पं च तत्तामसमुदाहृतम् ॥१८- २२॥

yattu kR^itsnavadekasminkArye saktamahaitukam.h .
atattvArthavadalpa.n cha tattAmasamudAhR^itam.h .. 18\-22..

yat.h = that which; tu = but; kR^itsnavat.h = as all in all; ekasmin.h = in one; kaarye = work; saktaM = attached; ahaitukaM = without cause; atattvaarthavat.h = without knowledge of reality; alpaM = very meagre; cha = and; tat.h = that; taamasaM = in the mode of darkness; udaahR^itaM = is said to be.

But that which clings to one single effect as if it were the whole, without concern for the cause, without grasping the real, and narrow is the example of Tamasik knowledge."

नियतं सङ्गरहितमरागद्वेषतः कृतम् ।
अफलप्रेप्सुना कर्म यत्तत्सात्त्विकमुच्यते ॥१८- २३॥

niyataM saN^garahitamarAgadveShataH kR^itam.h .
aphalaprepsunA karma yattatsAttvikamuchyate .. 18\-23..

niyataM = regulated; saN^garahitaM = without attachment; araagadveshhataH = without love or hatred; kR^itaM = done; aphalaprepsunaa = by one without desire for fruitive result; karma = action; yat.h = which; tat.h = that; saattvikaM = Satvika; uchyate = is called.

Actions ordained without attachment, devoid of likes & dislikes; and by the one who does not desire fruit is said to be Saattvika. (18.23)

यत्तु कामेप्सुना कर्म साहंकारेण वा पुनः ।
क्रियते बहुलायासं तद्राजसमुदाहृतम् ॥१८- २४॥

yattu kAmepsunA karma sAha.nkAreNa vA punaH .
kriyate bahulAyAsaM tadrAjasamudAhR^itam.h .. 18\-24..

yat.h = that which; tu = but; kaamepsunaa = by one with desires for fruitive results; karma = work; saahaN^kaareNa = with ego; vaa = or; punaH = again; kriyate = is performed; bahulaayaasaM = with great labor; tat.h = that; raajasaM = Rajasik udaahR^itaM = is said to be.

Action performed with selfish motives, or again with ego, and with much effort; is declared to be Raajasika. (18.24)

अनुबन्धं क्षयं हिंसामनपेक्ष्य च पौरुषम् ।
मोहादारभ्यते कर्म यत्तत्तामसमुच्यते ॥१८- २५॥

anubandha.n kShayaM hi.nsAmanapekShya cha pauruSham.h .
mohAdArabhyate karma yattattAmasamuchyate .. 18\-25..

anubandhaM = of future bondage; kshayaM = destruction; hi.nsaaM = and distress to others; anapekshya = without considering the consequences; cha = also; paurushhaM = self-sanctioned; mohaat.h = by illusion; aarabhyate = is begun; karma = work; yat.h = which; tat.h = that; taamasaM = Tamasik; uchyate = is said to be.

Action that is undertaken because of delusion; disregarding consequences, loss or injury to others, as well as one's own ability is said to be Taamasika action. (18.25)

मुक्तसङ्गोऽनहंवादी धृत्युत्साहसमन्वितः ।
सिद्ध्यसिद्ध्योर्निर्विकारः कर्ता सात्त्विक उच्यते ॥१८- २६॥

muktasaN^go.anaha.nvAdI dhR^ityutsAhasamanvitaH .
sid.hdhyasid.hdhyornirvikAraH kartA sAttvika uchyate .. 18\-26..

muktasaN^gaH = liberated from all material association; anaha.nvaadi = without false ego; dhR^iti = with determination; utsaaha = and great enthusiasm; samanvitaH = qualified; siddhi = in perfection; asid.hdhyoH = and failure; nirvikaaraH = without change; kartaa = worker; saattvikaH = Satvik; uchyate = is said to be.

The agent who is free from attachment, is non-egotistic, endowed with resolve and enthusiasm, and unperturbed in success or failure is called Saattvika. (18.26)

रागी कर्मफलप्रेप्सुर्लुब्धो हिंसात्मकोऽशुचिः ।
हर्षशोकान्वितः कर्ता राजसः परिकीर्तितः ॥१८- २७॥
rAgI karmaphalaprepsurlubdho hi.nsAtmako.ashuchiH .
harShashokAnvitaH kartA rAjasaH parikIrtitaH .. 18\-27..

raagii = very much attached; karmaphala = the fruit of the work; prepsuH = desiring; lubdhaH = greedy; hi.nsaatmakaH = harmful nature; ashuchiH = unclean; harshhashokaanvitaH = subject to joy and sorrow; kartaa = such a worker; raajasaH = Rajasik; parikiirtitaH = is declared.

one who is passionate, desires the fruits of work, who is greedy,violent, impure, and is affected by joy and sorrow; such an agent is proclaimed to be Raajasika. (18.27)

अयुक्तः प्राकृतः स्तब्धः शठो नैष्कृतिकोऽलसः ।
विषादी दीर्घसूत्री च कर्ता तामस उच्यते ॥१८- २८॥
ayuktaH prAkR^itaH stabdhaH shaTho naiShkR^itiko.alasaH .
viShAdI dIrghasUtrI cha kartA tAmasa uchyate .. 18\-28..

ayuktaH = not referring to the scriptural injunctions; praakR^itaH = materialistic; stabdhaH = obstinate; shaThaH = deceitful; naishhkR^itikaH = expert in insulting others; alasaH = lazy; vishhaadi = morose; diirghasuutrii = procrastinating; cha = also; kartaa = worker; taamasaH = in the mode of ignorance; uchyate = is said to be.

Undisciplined, vulgar, stubborn, wicked, malicious, lazy, depressed, and procrastinating; such an agent is called a Taamasika agent. (18.28)

बुद्धेर्भेदं धृतेश्चैव गुणतस्त्रिविधं शृणु ।
प्रोच्यमानमशेषेण पृथक्त्वेन धनञ्जय ॥१८- २९॥
buddherbhedaM dhR^iteshchaiva guNatastrividhaM shR^iNu .
prochyamAnamasheSheNa pR^ithaktvena dhana~njaya .. 18\-29..

buddheH = of intelligence; bhedaM = the differences; dhR^iteH = of steadiness; cha = also; eva = certainly; guNataH = by the modes of material nature; trividhaM = of three kinds; shR^iNu = just hear; prochyamaanaM = as described by Me; asheshheNa = in detail; pR^ithaktvena = differently;dhanaJNjaya = O winner of wealth.

Now hear the threefold division of intellect and resolve, based on Gunas, as explained by Me fully and separately, O Arjuna. (18.29)

प्रवृत्तिं च निवृत्तिं च कार्याकार्ये भयाभये ।
बन्धं मोक्षं च या वेत्ति बुद्धिः सा पार्थ सात्त्विकी ॥१८- ३०॥

pravR^itti.n cha nivR^itti.n cha kAryAkArye bhayAbhaye .
bandhaM mokSha.n cha yA vetti buddhiH sA pArtha sAttvikI .. 18\-30

pravR^ittiM = doing; cha = also; nivR^ittiM = not doing; cha = and; kaarya = what ought to be done; akaarye = and what ought not to be done; bhaya = fear; abhaye = and fearlessness; bandhaM = bondage; mokshaM = liberation; cha = and; yaa = that which; vetti = knows; buddhiH = understanding; saa = that; paartha = O son of Pritha; saattvikii = Satvika.

That which knows action and inaction, what ought to be done and what ought not to be done, fear and absence of fear, bondage and liberation, that intellect is Sattvic, O Arjuna (Partha). (18.30)

यया धर्ममधर्मं च कार्यं चाकार्यमेव च ।
अयथावत्प्रजानाति बुद्धिः सा पार्थ राजसी ॥१८- ३१॥

yayA dharmamadharma.n cha kArya.n chAkAryameva cha
.
ayathAvatprajAnAti buddhiH sA pArtha rAjasI .. 18\-31..

yayaa = by which; harmaM = the principles of religion; adharmaM = irreligion; cha = and; kaaryaM = what ought to be done; cha = also; akaaryaM = what ought not to be done; eva = certainly; cha = also; ayathaavat.h = imperfectly; prajaanaati = knows; buddhiH = intelligence; saa = that; paartha = O son of Pritha; raajasii = Rajasik.

The intellect by which one incorrectly distinguishes between Dharma and Adharma, and right and wrong action; that intellect is Raajasika, O Partha (Arjuna). (18.31)

अधर्मं धर्ममिति या मन्यते तमसावृता ।
सर्वार्थान्विपरीतांश्च बुद्धिः सा पार्थ तामसी ॥१८- ३२॥

adharma.n dharmamiti yA manyate tamasAvR^itA .
sarvArthAnviparItA.nshcha buddhiH sA pArtha tAmasI .. 18\-32..

adharmaM = irreligion; dharmaM = religion; iti = thus; yaa = which; manyate = thinks; tamasa = by illusion; aavR^itaa = covered; sarvaarthaan.h = all things; vipariitaan.h = in the wrong direction; cha = also; buddhiH = intelligence; saa = that; paartha = O son of Pritha; taamasii = Tamasik.

That which, enwrapped in darkness, thinks Wrong to be Right, and sees all things contrary to truth, that Reason O Partha, is of Tamasik. (18.32)

धृत्या यया धारयते मनःप्राणेन्द्रियक्रियाः ।
योगेनाव्यभिचारिण्या धृतिः सा पार्थ सात्त्विकी ॥१८- ३३॥

dhR^ityA yayA dhArayate manaHprANendriyakriyAH .
yogenAvyabhichAriNyA dhR^itiH sA pArtha sAttvikI .. 18\-33..

dhR^ityaa = determination; yayaa = by which; dhaarayate = one restrains; manaH = of the mind; praaNa = life, breath; indriya = and senses; kriyaaH = the activities; yogena = by yoga practice; avyabhichaariNyaa = without any break; dhR^itiH = determination; saa = that; paartha = O son of Pritha; saattvikii = Satvika.

The resolve by which one regulates the activities of mind, breath, and senses through unwavering practice of yoga, is Saattvika, O Arjuna. (18.33)

यया तु धर्मकामार्थान्धृत्या धारयतेऽर्जुन ।
प्रसङ्गेन फलाकाङ्क्षी धृतिः सा पार्थ राजसी ॥१८- ३४॥

yayA tu dharmakAmArthAndhR^ityA dhArayate.arjuna .
prasaN^gena phalAkAN^kShI dhR^itiH sA pArtha rAjasI .. 18\-34..

yayaa = by which; tu = but; dharma = religiosity; kaama = sense gratification; arthan.h = and economic development; dhR^itya = Resolve; dhaarayate = one restrains ; arjuna = O Arjuna; prasaN^gena = because of attachment; phalaakaaN^kshii = desiring fruitive results; dhR^itiH = resolve; saa = that; paartha = O son of Pritha; raajasii = Rajasik.

The resolve by which a person, craving for the fruits of work, clings to Dharma or righteous deeds, Artha or accumulation of wealth, and Kaama or enjoyment of sensual pleasures with great attachment; that resolve, O Arjuna, is Raajasika. (18.34)

यया स्वप्नं भयं शोकं विषादं मदमेव च ।
न विमुञ्चति दुर्मेधा धृतिः सा पार्थ तामसी ॥१८- ३५॥

yayA svapnaM bhayaM shokaM viShAdaM madameva cha
.
na vimu~nchati durmedhA dhR^itiH sA pArtha tAmasI .. 18\-35..

yayaa = by which; svapnaM = dreaming; bhayaM = fearfulness; shokaM = lamentation; vishhaadaM = moroseness; madaM = illusion; eva = certainly; cha = also; na = never; vimuJNchati = one gives up; durmedhaa = unintelligent; dhR^itiH = determination; saa = that; paartha = O son of Pritha; taamasii = in the mode of ignorance.

That by which one from stupidity does not abandon sleep, fear, grief, despair, and also illusion, that resolve, O Partha, is dark.(18.35)

सुखं त्विदानीं त्रिविधं शृणु मे भरतर्षभ ।
अभ्यासाद्रमते यत्र दुःखान्तं च निगच्छति ॥१८- ३६॥

sukhaM tvidAnI.n trividhaM shR^iNu me bharatarShabha .
abhyAsAdramate yatra duHkhAnta.n cha nigachchhati .. 18\-36.

sukhaM = happiness; tu = but; idaaniiM = now; trividhaM = of three kinds; shR^iNu = hear; me = from Me; bharatarshhabha = O best amongst the Bharatas; abhyaasaat.h = by practice; ramate = one enjoys; yatra = where; duHkha = of distress; antaM = the end; cha = also; nigachchhati = gains.

And now hear from Me, O Arjuna, about the threefold pleasure. The practice of which results in cessation of sorrow. (18.36)

यत्तदग्रे विषमिव परिणामेऽमृतोपमम् ।
तत्सुखं सात्त्विकं प्रोक्तमात्मबुद्धिप्रसादजम् ॥१८- ३७॥

yattadagre viShamiva pariNAme.amR^itopamam.h .

tatsukhaM sAttvikaM proktamAtmabuddhiprasAdajam.h .. 18\-37..

yat.h = which; tat.h = that; agre = in the beginning; vishhamiva = like poison; pariNaame = at the end; amR^ita = nectar; upamaM = compared to; tat.h = that; sukhaM = happiness; saattvikaM = in the mode of goodness; proktaM = is said; aatma = in the self; buddhi = of intelligence; prasaadajaM = born of the satisfaction.

The pleasure which appears as poison in the beginning but is like nectar in the end, comes by the grace of Self-knowledge; is good or Saattvika. (18.37)

विषयेन्द्रियसंयोगाद्यत्तदग्रेऽमृतोपमम् |
परिणामे विषमिव तत्सुखं राजसं स्मृतम् ||१८- ३८||

viShayendriyasa.nyogAdyattadagre.amR^itopamam.h .
pariNAme viShamiva tatsukhaM rAjasaM smR^itam.h .. 18\-38..

vishhaya = of the objects of the senses; indriya = and the senses; sa.nyogaat.h = from the combination; yat.h = which; tat.h = that; agre = in the beginning; amR^itopamaM = just like nectar; pariNaame = at the end; vishhamiva = like poison; tat.h = that; sukhaM = happiness; raajasaM = in the mode of passion; smR^itaM = is considered.

Pleasure originating from the indulgence of sense organs with the objects of senses appear as nectar in the beginning, but becomes poison in the end is called Raajasika pleasure. (18.38)

यदग्रे चानुबन्धे च सुखं मोहनमात्मनः |
निद्रालस्यप्रमादोत्थं तत्तामसमुदाहृतम् ||१८- ३९||

yadagre chAnubandhe cha sukhaM mohanamAtmanaH .
nidrAlasyapramAdottha.n tattAmasamudAhR^itam.h .. 18\-39..

yat.h = that which; agre = in the beginning; cha = also; anubandhe = at the end; cha = also; sukhaM = happiness; mohanaM = illusory; aatmanaH = of the self; nidraa = sleep; aalasya = laziness; pramaada = and illusion; utthaM = produced of; tat.h = that; taamasaM = in the mode of ignorance; udaahR^itaM = is said to be.

Pleasure that deludes a person in the beginning and in the end; which comes from sleep, laziness, and confusion; such pleasure is called Taamasika (pleasure). (18.39)

न तदस्ति पृथिव्यां वा दिवि देवेषु वा पुनः ।
सत्त्वं प्रकृतिजैर्मुक्तं यदेभिः स्यात्त्रिभिर्गुणैः ॥१८- ४०॥

na tadasti pR^ithivyA.n vA divi deveShu vA punaH .
sattvaM prakR^itijairmukta.n yadebhiH syAttribhirguNaiH .. 18\-40..

na = not; tat.h = that; asti = there is; pR^ithivyaaM = on the earth; vaa = or; divi = in the higher planetary system; deveshhu = amongst the demigods; vaa = or; punaH = again; sattvaM = existence; prakR^itijaiH = born of material nature; muktaM = liberated; yat.h = that; ebhiH = from the influence of these; syaat.h = is; tribhiH = three; guNaiH = modes of material nature.

There is no being, either on the earth or in the heaven or among the divines, who is free from these three Gunas of Prakriti, the material nature. (18.40)

ब्राह्मणक्षत्रियविशां शूद्राणां च परन्तप ।
कर्माणि प्रविभक्तानि स्वभावप्रभवैर्गुणैः ॥१८- ४१॥

brAhmaNakShatriyavishA.n shUdrANA.n cha parantapa .
karmANi pravibhaktAni svabhAvaprabhavairguNaiH .. 18\-41..

braahmaNa = of the brahmanas; kshatriya = the ksatriyas; vishaaM = and the vaisyas; shuudraaNaaM = of the shudras; cha = and; parantapa = O subduer of the enemies; karmaaNi = the activities; pravibhaktaani = are divided; svabhaava = their own nature; prabhavaiH = born of; guNaiH = by the attribute.

Of Brahmanas and Kshatriyas and Vaisyas, as also of Sudras, 0 Parantapa, the duties are divided according to the qualities born of nature.(18.41) ; (may also refer 4.13)

शमो दमस्तपः शौचं क्षान्तिरार्जवमेव च ।
ज्ञानं विज्ञानमास्तिक्यं ब्रह्मकर्म स्वभावजम् ॥१८- ४२॥

shamo damastapaH shauchaM kShAntirArjavameva cha .
GYAnaM viGYAnamAstikyaM brahmakarma svabhAvajam.h .. 18\-42..

samaH = peacefulness; damaH = self-control; tapaH = austerity; shauchaM = purity; kshaantiH = tolerance; aarjavaM = honesty; eva = certainly; cha = and; GYaanaM = knowledge; viGYaanaM = wisdom; aastikyaM = belief in God; brahma = of a Brahmana; karma = duty; svabhaavajaM = born of his own nature.

Serenity, self-restraint, austerity, purity, forgiveness and also uprightness, wisdom, knowledge, belief in God, are the Brahmana duty, born of his own nature. (18.42)

शौर्यं तेजो धृतिर्दाक्ष्यं युद्धे चाप्यपलायनम् ।
दानमीश्वरभावश्च क्षात्रं कर्म स्वभावजम् ॥१८- ४३॥

shaurya.n tejo dhR^itirdAkShya.n yuddhe chApyapalAyanam.h .
dAnamIshvarabhAvashcha kShAtraM karma svabhAvajam.h .. 18\-43..

shauryaM = heroism; tejaH = power; dhR^itiH = determination; daakshyaM = resourcefulness; yuddhe = in battle; cha = and; api = also; apalaayanaM = not fleeing; daanaM = generosity; iishvara = of leadership; bhaavaH = the nature; cha = and; kshaatraM = of a ksatriya; karma = duty; svabhaavajaM = born of his own nature.

Those having the qualities of heroism, vigor, resolve, dexterity, not fleeing from battle, charity, enerosity, the nature of a ruler, are the Kshattriya duty, born of his own nature.. (18.43)

कृषिगौरक्ष्यवाणिज्यं वैश्यकर्म स्वभावजम् ।
परिचर्यात्मकं कर्म शूद्रस्यापि स्वभावजम् ॥१८- ४४॥

kR^iShigaurakShyavANijya.n vaishyakarma svabhAvajam.h .
paricharyAtmakaM karma shUdrasyApi svabhAvajam.h .. 18\-44..

kR^ishhi = plowing; go = of cows; rakshya = protection; vaaNijyaM = trade; vaishya = of a vaisya; karma = duty; svabhaavajaM = born of his own nature; paricharya = service; atmakaM = consisting of; karma = duty; shuudrasya = of the shudra; api = also; svabhaavajaM = born of his own nature.

Ploughing, protection of kine, and trade are the Vaishya duty, born of his own nature. Action of the nature of service is the Shudra duty , born of his own nature.(18.44)

स्वे स्वे कर्मण्यभिरतः संसिद्धिं लभते नरः ।
स्वकर्मनिरतः सिद्धिं यथा विन्दति तच्छृणु ॥१८- ४५॥

sve sve karmaNyabhirataH sa.nsiddhi.n labhate naraH .
svakarmanirataH siddhi.n yathA vindati tachchhR^iNu .. 18\-45..

sve sve = each his own; karmaNi = work; abhirataH = following; sa.nsiddhiM = perfection; labhate = achieves; naraH = a man; svakarma = in his own duty; nirataH = engaged; siddhiM = perfection; yathaa = as; vindati = attains; tat.h = that; shR^iNu = listen.

Deeply engrossed in their own work, man achieves perfection; Listen to Me how one attains perfection while engaged in one's own work. (18.45)

यतः प्रवृत्तिर्भूतानां येन सर्वमिदं ततम् ।
स्वकर्मणा तमभ्यर्च्य सिद्धिं विन्दति मानवः ॥१८- ४६॥

yataH pravR^ittirbhUtAnA.n yena sarvamidaM tatam.h .
svakarmaNA tamabhyarchya siddhi.n vindati mAnavaH .. 18\-46..

yataH = from whom; pravR^ittiH = the emanation; bhuutaanaaM = this world ; yena = by whom; sarvaM = all; idaM = this; tataM = is pervaded; svakarmaNaa = by his own duties; taM = Him; abhyarchya = by worshiping; siddhiM = perfection; vindati = achieves; maanavaH = a man.

He from whom all beings originate, and by whom all this universe is pervaded; by performing one's own duty, thus worshipping Him one attains perfection. (18.46)

श्रेयान्स्वधर्मो विगुणः परधर्मात्स्वनुष्ठितात् ।
स्वभावनियतं कर्म कुर्वन्नाप्नोति किल्बिषम् ॥१८- ४७॥

shreyAnsvadharmo viguNaH paradharmAtsvanuShThitAt.h .
svabhAvaniyataM karma kurvannApnoti kilbiSham.h .. 18\-47..

shreyaan.h = better; svadharmaH = one's own occupation; viguNaH = imperfectly performed; paradharmaat.h = than; another's occupation; svanushhThitaat.h = perfectly done; svabhaavaniyataM = prescribed according to one's nature; karma = work; kurvan.h =

performing; na = never; aapnoti = achieves; kilbishaM = sinful reactions.

Better is one's own work according to one's own nature even if not well performed, than the work of another's nature well performed. Doing the duty ordained according to nature one incurs no sin. (See also 3.35) (18.47)

सहजं कर्म कौन्तेय सदोषमपि न त्यजेत् ।
सर्वारम्भा हि दोषेण धूमेनाग्निरिवावृताः ॥१८- ४८॥

sahajaM karma kaunteya sadoShamapi na tyajet.h .
sarvArambhA hi doSheNa dhUmenAgnirivAvR^itAH .. 18\-48..

sahajaM = natural; karma = work; kaunteya = O son of Kunti; sadoshhaM = with fault; api = although; na = never; tyajet.h = one should give up; sarvaarambhaH = all ventures; hi = certainly; doshhena = with fault; dhuumena = with smoke; agniH = fire; iva = as; aavR^itaaH = covered.

One's natural work, even though defective, should not be abandoned; because all undertakings are enveloped by defects as fire is covered by smoke, O Arjuna. (18.48)

असक्तबुद्धिः सर्वत्र जितात्मा विगतस्पृहः ।
नैष्कर्म्यसिद्धिं परमां संन्यासेनाधिगच्छति ॥१८- ४९॥

asaktabuddhiH sarvatra jitAtmA vigataspR^ihaH .
naiShkarmyasiddhiM paramA.n sa.nnyAsenAdhigachchhati .. 18\-49..

asaktabuddhiH = having unattached intelligence; sarvatra = everywhere; jitaatmaa = having control of the mind; vigataspR^ihaH = without material desires; naishhkarmyasiddhiM = as if he has abandoned all work; paramaaM = supreme; sa.nnyaasena = by the renounced order of life; adhigachchhati = one attains.

With mind free from attachment, everyehere having control of mind, free from material desires, attains the supreme perfection of freedom from (the bondage of) Karma through renunciation. (18.49)

सिद्धिं प्राप्तो यथा ब्रह्म तथाप्नोति निबोध मे ।
समासेनैव कौन्तेय निष्ठा ज्ञानस्य या परा ॥१८- ५०॥

siddhiM prApto yathA brahma tathApnoti nibodha me .

samAsenaiva kaunteya niShThA GYAnasya yA parA .. 18\-50..

siddhiM = perfection; praaptaH = achieving; yathaa = as; brahma = the Supreme; tathaa = so; aapnoti = one; achieves; nibodha = try to understand; me = from Me; samaasena = briefly; eva = certainly; kaunteya = O son of Kunti; nishhThaa = the stage; GYaanasya = of knowledge; yaa = which; paraa = transcendental.

How he who has attained perfection obtains the eternal Supreme, that highest state of wisdom learn from Me succinctly, O Kaunteya. (18.50)

बुद्ध्या विशुद्धया युक्तो धृत्यात्मानं नियम्य च |
शब्दादीन्विषयांस्त्यक्त्वा रागद्वेषौ व्युदस्य च ||१८- ५१||

bud.hdhyA vishuddhayA yukto dhR^ityAtmAnaM niyamya cha .
shabdAdInviShayA.nstyaktvA rAgadveShau vyudasya cha .. 18\-51..

bud.hdhyaa = with the intelligence; vishuddhayaa = fully purified; yuktaH = engaged; dhR^itya = by determination; aatmaanaM = the self; niyamya = regulating; cha = also; shabdaadin.h = such as sound; vishhayaan.h = the sense objects; tyaktvaa = giving up; raaga = attachment; dveshhau = and hatred; vyudasya = laying aside; cha = also.

Endowed with purified intellect, subduing oneself with resolve, turning away from sound and other objects of the sense gratification, giving up likes and dislikes; and (18.51)

विविक्तसेवी लघ्वाशी यतवाक्कायमानसः |
ध्यानयोगपरो नित्यं वैराग्यं समुपाश्रितः ||१८- ५२||

viviktasevI laghvAshI yatavAkkAyamAnasaH .
dhyAnayogaparo nitya.n vairAgya.n samupAshritaH .. 18\-52..

viviktasevii = living in a secluded place; laghvaashii = eating a small quantity; yata = having controlled; vaak.h = speech; kaaya = body; maanasaH = and mind; dhyaanayogaparaH = absorbed in meditation; nityaM = always; vairaagyaM = detachment; samupaashritaH = having taken shelter of.

Dwelling in solitude, eating but little, controlling speech, body and mind, and ever engaged in meditation and concentration and taking refuge in dispassion. (18.52)

अहंकारं बलं दर्पं कामं क्रोधं परिग्रहम् ।
विमुच्य निर्ममः शान्तो ब्रह्मभूयाय कल्पते ॥१८- ५३॥
aha.nkAraM balaM darpa.n kAmaM krodhaM parigraham.h
.
vimuchya nirmamaH shAnto brahmabhUyAya kalpate .. 18\-53..

ahaN^kaaraM = false ego; balaM = false strength; darpaM = false pride; kaamaM = lust; krodhaM = anger; parigrahaM = possession ; vimuchya = being delivered from; nirmamaH = without a sense of proprietorship; shaantaH = peaceful; brahmabhuuyaaya = for self-realization; kalpate = is qualified.

And casting aside ego, force, arrogance, desire, anger, possession; egoless and tranquil in mind, he becomes worthy of becoming one with Brahman.(18.53)

ब्रह्मभूतः प्रसन्नात्मा न शोचति न काङ्क्षति ।
समः सर्वेषु भूतेषु मद्भक्तिं लभते पराम् ॥१८- ५४॥
brahmabhUtaH prasannAtmA na shochati na kAN^kShati .
samaH sarveShu bhUteShu madbhakti.n labhate parAm.h .. 18\-54..

brahmabhuutaH = being one with the Absolute; prasannaatmaa = fully joyful; na = never; shochati = laments; na = never; kaaN^kshati = desires; samaH = equally disposed; sarveshhu = to all; bhuuteshhu = living entities; mad.hbhaktiM = my part; labhate = gains; paraaM = transcendental.

Being one with the Absolute (Brahm), the serene one neither grieves nor desires; treating all beings alike, one becomes a part of Me. (18.54)

भक्त्या मामभिजानाति यावान्यश्चास्मि तत्त्वतः ।
ततो मां तत्त्वतो ज्ञात्वा विशते तदनन्तरम् ॥१८- ५५॥
bhaktyA mAmabhijAnAti yAvAnyashchAsmi tattvataH .
tato mAM tattvato GYAtvA vishate tadanantaram.h .. 18\-55..

bhaktyaa = by becoming my part; maaM = Me; abhijaanaati = one can know; yaavaan.h = as much as yah; chaasmi = as I am. tattvataH = in truth; tataH = thereafter; maaM = Me; tattvataH = in truth; GYaatvaa = knowing; vishate = he enters; tadanantaraM = thereafter.

By becoming my part, he knows Me (Lord), who am I (who the SupremLord is?) in essence; Thus knowing me in essence, he immediately merges into me. (18.55)

सर्वकर्माण्यपि सदा कुर्वाणो मद्व्यपाश्रयः |
मत्प्रसादादवाप्नोति शाश्वतं पदमव्ययम् ||१८- ५६||

sarvakarmANyapi sadA kurvANo mad.hvyapAshrayaH .
matprasAdAdavApnoti shAshvataM padamavyayam.h .. 18\-56..

sarva = all; karmaaNi = activities; api = although; sadaa = always; kurvaaNaH = performing; mad.hvyapaashrayaH = under My protection; matprasaadaat.h = by My mercy; avaapnoti = one achieves; shaashvataM = the eternal; padaM = abode; avyayaM = imperishable.

Doing all actions always under My protection; by My (Lord's) grace he gets the eternal, imperishable abode.(18.56)

चेतसा सर्वकर्माणि मयि संन्यस्य मत्परः |
बुद्धियोगमुपाश्रित्य मच्चित्तः सततं भव ||१८- ५७||

chetasA sarvakarmANi mayi sa.nnyasya matparaH .
buddhiyogamupAshritya machchittaH satataM bhava .. 18\-57..

chetasaa = Conciously; sarvakarmaaNi = all kinds of activities; mayi = unto Me; sa.nnyasya = giving up; matparaH = under My protection; buddhiyogaM = the Yoga of intellect; upaashritya = taking shelter of; machchittaH = bring awareness upon me; satataM = continuously; bhava = just become.

Renouncing consciously all actions to Me, by yoga of intellect, bring your awareness incessantly on me. (18.57)

मच्चित्तः सर्वदुर्गाणि मत्प्रसादात्तरिष्यसि |
अथ चेत्त्वमहंकारान्न श्रोष्यसि विनङ्क्ष्यसि ||१८- ५८||

machchittaH sarvadurgANi matprasAdAttariShyasi .

atha chettvamaha.nkArAnna shroShyasi vinaN^kShyasi .. 18\-58..

mat.h = of Me; chittaH = awareness; sarva = all; durgaaNi = impediments; matprasaadaat.h = by My mercy; tarishhyasi = you will overcome; atha = but; chet.h = if; tvaM = you; ahaN^kaaraat.h = by false ego; na shrosyasi = do not hear; vinaN^kshyasi = you will be lost.

Thus bringing your awareness on me you will overcome all difficulties by my grace. But, if you do not listen to Me due to ego, you shall perish. (18.58)

यदहंकारमाश्रित्य न योत्स्य इति मन्यसे ।
मिथ्यैष व्यवसायस्ते प्रकृतिस्त्वां नियोक्ष्यति ॥१८- ५९॥

yadaha.nkAramAshritya na yotsya iti manyase .
mithyaiSha vyavasAyaste prakR^itistvA.n niyokShyati .. 18\-59..

yat.h = if; ahaN^kaaraM = of false ego; aashritya = taking shelter; na yotsye = I shall not fight; iti = thus; manyase; = you think; mithyaishhaH = this is all false; vyavasaayaH = business; te = your; prakR^itiH = material nature; tvaaM = you; niyokshyati = will engage.

If due to ego you think: I shall not fight; this resolve of yours is vain. Your own nature will compel you to fight. (18.59)

स्वभावजेन कौन्तेय निबद्धः स्वेन कर्मणा ।
कर्तुं नेच्छसि यन्मोहात्करिष्यस्यवशोपि तत् ॥१८- ६०॥

svabhAvajena kaunteya nibaddhaH svena karmaNA .
kartuM nechchhasi yanmohAtkariShyasyavashopi tat.h .. 18\-60..

svabhaavajena = born of your own nature; kaunteya = O son of Kunti; nibaddhaH = conditioned; svena = by your own; karmaNaa = activities; kartuM = to do; na = not; ichchhasi = you like; yat.h = that which; mohaat.h = by illusion; karishhyasi = you will do; avashaH = involuntarily; api = even; tat.h = that.

What you do not wish to do; you shall do even that against your will, out of delusion, bound by your own nature-born Karma, O Arjuna.(18.60)

ईश्वरः सर्वभूतानां हृद्देशेऽर्जुन तिष्ठति ।
भ्रामयन्सर्वभूतानि यन्त्रारूढानि मायया ॥१८- ६१॥

IshvaraH sarvabhUtAnA.n hR^iddeshe.arjuna tiShThati .
bhrAmayansarvabhUtAni yantrArUDhAni mAyayA .. 18\-61..

iishvaraH = the Supreme Lord; sarvabhuutaanaaM = of all living entities; hR^iddeshe = in the location of the heart; arjuna = O Arjuna; tishhThati = resides; bhraamayan.h = causing to travel; sarvabhuutaanii = all living entities; yantra = on a machine; aaruuDhaani = being placed; maayayaa = under the spell of material energy.

The Lord abides in the heart of all beings, O Arjuna, causing all beings to act by His power of Maya as if they are mounted on a machine. (18.61)

तमेव शरणं गच्छ सर्वभावेन भारत।
तत्प्रसादात्परां शान्तिं स्थानं प्राप्स्यसि शाश्वतम् ॥१८- ६२॥

tameva sharaNaM gachchha sarvabhAvena bhArata .
tatprasAdAtparAM shAntiM sthAnaM prApsyasi shAshvatam.h .. 18\-62..

taM = unto Him; eva = certainly; sharaNam gachchha = surrender; sarvabhaavena = in all respects; bhaarata = O son of Bharata; tatprasaadaat.h = by His grace; paraaM = transcendental; shaantiM = peace; sthaanaM = the abode; praapsyasi = you will get; shaashvataM = eternal.

Seek refuge in Him alone with all your heart, O Arjuna. By His grace you shall attain supreme peace and the eternal abode. (18.62)

इति ते ज्ञानमाख्यातं गुह्याद्गुह्यतरं मया।
विमृश्यैतदशेषेण यथेच्छसि तथा कुरु ॥१८- ६३॥

iti te GYAnamAkhyAtaM guhyAd.hguhyataraM mayA .
vimR^ishyaitadasheSheNa yathechchhasi tathA kuru .. 18\-63..

iti = thus; te = unto you; GYaanaM = knowledge; aakhyaataM = described; guhyaat.h = than confidential; guhyataraM = still more confidential; mayaa = by Me; vimR^ishya = deliberating; etat.h = on this; asheshheNa = fully; yathaa = as; ichchhasi = you like; tathaa = that; kuru = perform.

Thus the knowledge that is more secret than the secret has been explained to you by Me. After fully reflecting on this, do as you wish. (18.63)

सर्वगुह्यतमं भूयः शृणु मे परमं वचः ।
इष्टोऽसि मे दृढमिति ततो वक्ष्यामि ते हितम् ॥१८- ६४॥

sarvaguhyatamaM bhUyaH shR^iNu me paramaM vachaH .
iShTo.asi me dR^iDhamiti tato vakShyAmi te hitam.h .. 18\-64..

sarvaguhyatamaM = the most confidential of all; bhuuyaH = again; shR^iNu = just hear; me = from Me; paramaM = the supreme; vachaH = instruction; ishhTaH asi = you are dear; me = to Me; dR^iDhaM = very; iti = thus; tataH = therefore; vakshyaami = I am speaking; te = for your; hitaM = benefit.

Hear again My supreme word, the most secret of all. You are very dear to Me, therefore, I shall tell this for your benefit. (18.64)

मन्मना भव मद्भक्तो मद्याजी मां नमस्कुरु ।
मामेवैष्यसि सत्यं ते प्रतिजाने प्रियोऽसि मे ॥१८- ६५॥

manmanA bhava madbhakto madyAjI mA.n namaskuru .
mAmevaiShyasi satya.n te pratijAne priyo.asi me .. 18\-65..

manmanaaH = thinking of Me; bhava = just become; mad.hbhaktaH = My devotee; madyaajii = My worshiper; maaM = unto Me; namaskuru = offer your obeisances; maaM = unto Me; eva = certainly; eshhyasi = you will come; satyaM = truly; te = to you; pratijaane = I promise; priyaH = dear; asi = you are; me = to Me.

Fix your mind on Me (Lord), be devoted to Me, worship Me, bow down to Me, and you shall certainly reach Me. I promise you because you are very dear to Me. (18.65)

सर्वधर्मान्परित्यज्य मामेकं शरणं व्रज ।
अहं त्वा सर्वपापेभ्यो मोक्षयिष्यामि मा शुचः ॥१८- ६६॥

sarvadharmAnparityajya mAmekaM sharaNaM vraja .
ahaM tvA sarvapApebhyo mokShayiShyAmi mA shuchaH .. 18\-66..

sarvadharmaan.h = all varieties of religion; parityajya = abandoning; maaM = unto Me; ekaM = only; sharaNaM = for surrender; vraja = go; ahaM = I; tvaaM = you; sarva = all; paapebhyaH = from sinful reactions; mokshayishhyaami = will deliver; maa = do not; shuchaH = worry.

Not caring about the righteous deeds, just surrender completely to Me (Supreme Lord). I shall liberate you from all sinful reactions. Do not grieve.(18.66)

इदं ते नातपस्काय नाभक्ताय कदाचन ।
न चाशुश्रूषवे वाच्यं न च मां योऽभ्यसूयति ॥१८- ६७॥

idaM te nAtapaskAya nAbhaktAya kadAchana .
na chAshushrUShave vAchya.n na cha mA.n yo.abhyasUyati .. 18\-67..

idaM = this; te = by you; na = never; atapaskaaya = to one who is not austere; na = never; abhaktaaya = to one who is not a devotee; kadaachana = at any time; na = never; cha = also; ashushruushhave = to one who is not; engaged in devotional service; vaachyaM = to be spoken; na = never; cha = also; maaM = toward Me; yaH = anyone who; abhyasuuyati = is envious.

This should never be spoken by you to one who is devoid of austerity, who is without devotion, who does not desire to listen, or who speaks ill of Me. (18.67)

य इदं परमं गुह्यं मद्भक्तेष्वभिधास्यति ।
भक्तिं मयि परां कृत्वा मामेवैष्यत्यसंशयः ॥१८- ६८॥

ya idaM paramaM guhyaM madbhakteShvabhidhAsyati .
bhaktiM mayi parAM kR^itvA mAmevaiShyatyasa.nshayaH .. 18\-68..
..

yaH = anyone who; idaM = this; paramaM = most; guhyaM = confidential secret; mat.h = of Mine; bhakteshhu = amongst devotees; abhidhaasyati = explains; bhaktiM = devotional service; mayi = unto Me; paraaM = transcendental; kR^itvaa = doing; maaM = unto Me; eva = certainly; eshhyati = comes ; asa.nshayaH = without doubt.

The one who describes this most secret knowledge amongst my devotees, thus showing highest devotion to me shall certainly come to me.(18.68)

न च तस्मान्मनुष्येषु कश्चिन्मे प्रियकृत्तमः ।
भविता न च मे तस्मादन्यः प्रियतरो भुवि ॥१८- ६९॥

na cha tasmAnmanuShyeShu kashchinme priyakR^ittamaH .
bhavitA na cha me tasmAdanyaH priyataro bhuvi .. 18\-69..

na = never; cha = and; tasmaat.h = than him; manushhyeshhu = among men; kashchit.h = anyone; me = to Me; priyakR^ittamaH = more dear; bhavitaa = will become; na = nor; cha = and; me = to Me; tasmaat.h = than him; anyaH = another; priyataraH = dearer; bhuvi = in this world.

No other person shall do a more pleasing service to Me, and no one on the earth shall be more dear to Me. (18.69)

अध्येष्यते च य इमं धर्म्यं संवादमावयोः ।
ज्ञानयज्ञेन तेनाहमिष्टः स्यामिति मे मतिः ॥१८- ७०॥

adhyeShyate cha ya imaM dharmya.n sa.nvAdamAvayoH .
GYAnayaGYena tenAhamiShTaH syAmiti me matiH .. 18\-70

adhyeshhyate = will study; cha = also; yaH = he who; imaM = this; dharmyaM = sacred; sa.nvaadaM = conversation; aavayoH = of ours; GYaana = of knowledge; yaGYena = by the sacrifice; tena = by him; ahaM = I; ishhTaH = worshiped; syaaM = shall be; iti = thus; me = My; matiH = opinion.

I shall be worshipped with Jnana-Yajna (or knowledge sacrifice) by those who shall study this sacred dialogue of ours. This is My opinion. (18.70)

श्रद्धावाननसूयश्च शृणुयादपि यो नरः ।
सोऽपि मुक्तः शुभाँल्लोकान्प्राप्नुयात्पुण्यकर्मणाम् ॥१८- ७१॥

arjuna uvAcha .
shraddhAvAnanasUyashcha shR^iNuyAdapi yo naraH .
so.api muktaH shubhA.NllokAnprApnuyAtpuNyakarmaNAm.h .. 18\-71..

shraddhaavaan.h = faithful; anasuuyaH = not envious; cha = and; shR^iNuyaat.h = does hear; api = certainly; yaH = who; naraH = a man; saH = he; api = also; muktaH = being liberated; shubhaan.h = the auspicious; lokaan.h = planets; praapnuyaat.h = he attains; puNyakarmaNaaM = of the pious.

Whoever hears this with faith and without cavil becomes free from sin, and attains heaven, abode of the pious . (18.71)

कच्चिदेतच्छ्रुतं पार्थ त्वयैकाग्रेण चेतसा ।
कच्चिदज्ञानसम्मोहः प्रनष्टस्ते धनञ्जय ॥१८- ७२॥

kachchidetachchhrutaM pArtha tvayaikAgreNa chetasA .

kachchidaGYAnasammohaH pranaShTaste dhana~njaya .. 18\-72..

kachchit.h = whether; etat.h = this; shrutaM = heard; paartha = O son of Pritha; tvayaa = by you; ekaagreNa = with full attention; chetasaa = by the mind; kachchit.h = whether; aGYaana = of ignorance; sammohaH = the illusion; praNashhTaH = dispelled; te = of you; dhanaJNjaya = O conqueror of wealth (Arjuna).

O Arjuna, did you listen to this with full attention? Has your delusion born of ignorance been destroyed? (18.72)

अर्जुन उवाच |
नष्टो मोहः स्मृतिर्लब्धा त्वत्प्रसादान्मयाच्युत |
स्थितोऽस्मि गतसन्देहः करिष्ये वचनं तव ||१८- ७३||

arjuna uvAcha .
naShTo mohaH smR^itirlabdhA tvatprasAdAnmayAchyuta .
sthito.asmi gatasandehaH kariShye vachanaM tava .. 18\-73..

arjuna uvaacha = Arjuna said; nashhTaH = dispelled; mohaH = illusion; smR^itiH = memory; labdhaa = regained; tvatprasaadaat.h = by Your mercy; mayaa = by me; achyuta = O infallible KRishhNa; sthitaH = situated; asmi = I am; gata = removed; sandehaH = all doubts; karishhye = I shall execute; vachanaM = order; tava = Your.

Arjuna said: By Your grace my delusion is destroyed, I have gained knowledge, my confusion is dispelled and I shall obey Your command. (18.73)

सञ्जय उवाच |
इत्यहं वासुदेवस्य पार्थस्य च महात्मनः |
संवादमिममश्रौषमद्भुतं रोमहर्षणम् ||१८- ७४||

sa~njaya uvAcha .
ityahaM vAsudevasya pArthasya cha mahAtmanaH .
sa.nvAdamimamashrauShamadbhutaM romaharShaNam.h .. 18\-74..

saJNjaya uvaacha = Sanjaya said; iti = thus; ahaM = I; vaasudevasya = of KRishhNa; paarthasya = and Arjuna; cha = also; mahaatmanaH = of the great soul; sa.nvaadaM = discussion; imaM =

this; ashraushhaM = have heard; adbhutaM = wonderful; romaharshhaNaM = making the hair stand on end.

Sanjaya said: Thus I heard this wonderful dialogue between Lord Krishna and Mahatma Arjuna, causing my hair to stand on end. (18.74)

व्यासप्रसादाच्छ्रुतवानेतद्गुह्यमहं परम् ।
योगं योगेश्वरात्कृष्णात्साक्षात्कथयतः स्वयम् ॥१८- ७५॥

vyAsaprasAdAchchhrutavAnetadguhyamahaM param.h .
yogaM yogeshvarAtkR^iShNAtsAkShAtkathayataH svayam.h .. 18\-75..

vyaasaprasaadaat.h = by the mercy of Vyasadeva; shrutavaan.h = have heard; etat.h = this; guhyaM = confidential; ahaM = I; paraM = the supreme; yogaM = mysticism; yogeshvaraat.h = from the master of all mysticism; kR^ishhNaat.h = from KRishhNa; saakshaat.h = directly; kathayataH = speaking; svayaM = personally.

By the grace of sage Vyaasa, I heard this most secret and supreme yoga directly from Krishna, the lord of yoga, Himself speaking before my very eyes. (18.75)

राजन्संस्मृत्य संस्मृत्य संवादमिममद्भुतम् ।
केशवार्जुनयोः पुण्यं हृष्यामि च मुहुर्मुहुः ॥१८- ७६॥

rAjansa.nsmR^itya sa.nsmR^itya sa.nvAdamimamadbhutam.h .
keshavArjunayoH puNyaM hR^iShyAmi cha muhurmuhuH .. 18\-76..

raajan.h = O King; sa.nsmR^itya = remembering; sa.nsmR^itya = remembering; sa.nvaadaM = message; imaM = this; adbhutaM = wonderful; keshava = of Lord KRishhNa; arjunayoH = and Arjuna; puNyaM = pious; hR^ishhyaami = I am taking pleasure; cha = also; muhurmuhuH = repeatedly.

O King, by repeated remembrance of this marvelous and sacred dialogue between Keshava (Lord Krishna) and Arjuna, I rejoice again and again. (18.76)

तच्च संस्मृत्य संस्मृत्य रूपमत्यद्भुतं हरेः ।
विस्मयो मे महान् राजन्हृष्यामि च पुनः पुनः ॥१८- ७७॥

tachcha sa.nsmR^itya sa.nsmR^itya rUpamatyadbhutaM hareH .

vismayo me mahAn.h rAjanhR^iShyAmi cha punaH punaH .. 18\-77..

tat.h = that; cha = also; sa.nsmR^itya = remembering; sa.nsmR^itya = remembering; ruupaM = form; ati = greatly; adbhutaM = wonderful; hareH = of Lord KRishhNa; vismayaH = wonder; me = my; mahaan.h = great; raajan.h = O King; hR^ishhyaami = I am enjoying; cha = also; punaH punaH = repeatedly.

Recollecting again and again, O King, that marvelous form of Krishna I am greatly amazed and I rejoice over and over again. (18.77)

यत्र योगेश्वरः कृष्णो यत्र पार्थो धनुर्धरः |
तत्र श्रीर्विजयो भूतिर्ध्रुवा नीतिर्मतिर्मम ||१८- ७८||

yatra yogeshvaraH kR^iShNo yatra pArtho dhanurdharaH .
tatra shrIrvijayo bhUtirdhruvA nItirmatirmama .. 18\-78..
AUM tatsaditi shrImadbhagavadgItAsUpaniShatsu

yatra = where; yogeshvaraH = the master of mysticism; kR^ishhNaH = Lord KRishhNa; yatra = where; paarthaH = the son of Pritha; dhanurdharaH = the carrier of the bow and arrow; tatra = there; shriiH = opulence; vijayaH = victory; bhuutiH = exceptional power; dhruvaa = certain; niitiH = morality; matirmama = my opinion

Wherever is Krishna, the lord of yoga; and wherever is Arjuna, the archer; there will be everlasting prosperity, victory, happiness, and morality. This is my conviction. (18.78)

ॐ तत्सदिति श्रीमद्भगवद्गीतासूपनिषत्सु
ब्रह्मविद्यायां योगशास्त्रे श्रीकृष्णार्जुनसंवादे
मोक्षसंन्यासयोगो नाम अष्टादशोऽध्यायः ||१८||

brahmavidyAyA.n yogashAstre
shrIkR^iShNArjunasa.nvAde
mokShasa.nnyAsayogo nAma aShTAdasho.adhyAyaH ..

अथाष्टादशोऽध्यायः | मोक्षसंन्यासयोगः

Epilogue

The purpose of the whole discourse of the Gita is to instil discriminative knowledge, so that one becomes capable of discriminating between right and wrong actions. Different people in the world follow diverse philosophies, religions and sects. They have their own beliefs and concepts of right and wrong actions. However, the Gita presents a litmus test to identify whether one is following the right path, irrespective of one's religion or sect, leading to the Absolute, so that one achieves the optimum blissful experience. In that way, the Gita is a secular treatise having universal appeal for all.

Right action comes through understanding the process of oneself. Self-knowledge is the beginning of wisdom required to understand the right action. The first six chapters of the Bhagavad-Gita gives an insight about the true nature of the self, which were discussed in the first volume titled "Understanding the Self". The Volume discussed about the knowledge of the true self that enables one to understand the impact of actions that will result in true happiness. Once the true nature of the self is understood, one is able to understand the kinds of actions, which would lead to perpetual pleasure, fulfilment and blissful state.

In second volume, titled "The Glimpses of the Absolute", the objective is to elucidate the true aspects of the God that are equally applicable to all religions and sects. Once a person is on the right way to acquire the true knowledge about the God, the person starts developing certain qualities as a result of his progress in right direction. Those qualities can serve as a touchstone to identify whether one is on a right path or not. As one progresses towards the Supreme, discriminative knowledge developed in the process serves as a flashlight to distinguish between right and wrong action.

Like you can approach a lighthouse from many direction along various paths, there is no unique path to achieve the Supreme. However, the increasing intensity of light along the direction one follows towards the lighthouse is an indicator of a right path. The Gita serves as a guide to acquaint us with the general principles applicable to all paths and define indicators that can aid one to understand one's progress.

The path of action, wherein one indulges in work without passionate desire for the result, but for the sake of work itself, immersing oneself completely in the work, focusing all attention to the job, deriving pleasure from the indulgence in work, leads one to the blissful position. Engaging in a work, in which its requirements perfectly match with the attributes and skills of a person gives immense satisfaction. The person doing such work absorbs himself completely in selfless actions as if absorbed in the Supreme. He reaches a non-dualistic state of consciousness in which the consciousness of the experiencing subject becomes one with the experienced object or work referred as Samadhi.

The path of knowledge is the path that lays emphasis on understanding the true nature of the Absolute. The path of knowledge tells us that all this world is pervaded by the higher nature of the God that is consciousness. The true un-manifested nature of the Supreme, the consciousness is beyond space and time dimensions that are familiar to our senses. The consciousness is the life force in all beings. This form is beyond the reach of the senses. In God, in his un-manifested form, dwell all beings. No being devoid of the consciousness can ever become an object of experience and therefore they dwell in the Supreme. However, as the consciousness, the Supreme is beyond the notion of space and time, strictly speaking, He cannot dwell in any being. The supreme is both connected, yet unattached from its own creation. The path of knowledge is difficult to understand as principles involved are complex and unfamiliar for the mind tuned to space time world.

In the path of Bhakti, one considers oneself a miniscule part of the Lord, who holds the complete cosmos and is the cause of life and death of all beings. For the follower of the path of bhakti she is a part of the all-encompassing Supreme, containing all the universe, the forces of nature and all beings. For her, the Lord is not formless, but has form and thus can be perceived by sense organs. Like herself, every being in the universe is part of the Supreme Lord. The Lord is master of the universe and everything is controlled by him and everything belongs to him. These simplified assumptions help the follower of the path of bhakti to understand the true formless nature of the supreme and also to reach the ultimate blissful position. A follower of Bhakti is always aware that her body is a part of a larger body called the planet, which is part of a much larger body called the solar system, which, in turn, is linked to the cosmos, and which is held together by the Lord himself.

A follower of Bhakti considers herself as an instrument of the God. She has no independent will of her own and surrenders herself to the command of the Supreme. Whatever she does is an action of the Lord, she merely being a tool in the hands of the Lord. For instance, Mother Teresa, in one of her interview conducted by Edward W. Desmond in 1989 for Time magazine said "I don't claim anything of the work. It's His work. I'm like a little pencil in His hand. That's all. He does the thinking. He does the writing. The pencil has nothing to do it. The pencil has only to be allowed to be used. In human terms, the success of our work should not have happened, no? That is a sign that it's His work, and that He is using others as instruments - all our Sisters. None of us could produce this. Yet see what He has done." Love for all exuded from her firm belief that Lord is present in every being. Mother Teresa used to say, "Seeking the face of God in everything, everyone, everywhere, all the time, and seeing his hand in every happening—that is contemplation in the heart of the world."

During the journey towards the Absolute through any path, the practitioner develops the qualities due to the grace of God regardless of her affiliations. Such a person hates nothing, not even that which causes her pain and regards all beings as herself. She is friendly and compassionate and does not regard anything as 'mine' and is free from egoism and her identity dissolves in the Ultimate. She is always content; thinking she has enough, whether she obtains or not the means of bodily sustenance. A person approaching towards the Absolute leaves every result of her actions to the Supreme and has no personal desires, therefore, the world is not agitated with her, and she is not agitated from the world, she is also free from anxieties of joy, anger and fear. Beyond love and hate, neither grieving nor desiring, renouncing good and evil both, treating alike foe and friend, also fame and ignominy, alike in cold and heat, pleasure and pain, devoid of attachment, treating praise and reproach equally, wholly content with whatever comes, having no attachment with the home, she is firm in mind.

Mahatma Gandhi, a Hindu by birth, was a staunch believer in love, nonviolence and truth. He never hated anybody, not even adversaries. He used to say "hate the sin not the sinner." Kabir, a 15th century Indian mystic poet, who is believed to be a Muslim by birth, suggested that True God is with the person who is on the path of righteousness, considered all creatures on earth as his own self, and who is passively detached from the affairs of the world. Although Mother Teresa, Kabir and Mahatma Gandhi, were from different religions, the qualities displayed by them confirm their march towards the Supreme according to the principles narrated in the Gita. The acts of the terrorists killing people in the name of their religion, on the other hand, clearly indicate that they are not on a path that leads to God.

One may be bewildered that how the philosophy that extolls love and equality for all and renunciation of the fruit of action, can advocate Arjun to fight the war. It may be noted that hating somebody may be a sin, nevertheless, despite every effort to settle an issue peacefully, not opposing an injustice is a greater sin. Killing your oppressor in a war in the interest of fairness and righteousness and hating him are two different things altogether. For instance, when you suffers from a problem in one part of your body, you make every effort to try to cure that part, if however, you fail to cure the diseased organ, in the interest of the wellbeing of the whole body you may decide to the surgically remove the afflicted part. However, deciding to surgically remove the afflicted part doesn't mean that you hate that part. Similarly, combating the injustice is necessary to retain the healthiness of the society and doesn't mean that you hate the person who is indulged in wrongdoing.

The principles expounded in the Bhagvad-Gita are applicable not only to assess the progress of individuals, but also the direction of the society. We have gone a long way since the time of caveman. But the question is, have we progressed in the right direction. There was an article in prestigious science journal "Nature" (dated 01- June-2017, page 73) that Humans are bringing about the sixth mass extinction of life on Earth, according to scientists writing in a special edition of the leading journal. Scientists say 25% of all mammals, 13% of birds are at risk as humans corner resources. "There is overwhelming evidence that habitat loss and fragmentation, over-exploitation of biological resources, pollution, species invasions and climate change have increased rates of global species extinctions to levels that are much higher than those observed in the fossil record." Yet these threats are not inevitable. Proactive international efforts to reduce consumption, minimize land clearing and habitat fragmentation, and protect natural lands could improve food security in developing nations and preserve much of Earth's remaining biodiversity.

The inability to identify oneself as a part of the whole macrocosm, the inability to identify one's true self as the self of all beings results in overexploitation of the biological resources and destruction of nature for short term benefits of the few, ultimately resulting in a situation where the humans themselves can no longer be sustained.

The present book, the third book in the series of "Demystifying the Bhagvad Gita" elaborates how the divine union of Parakriti and Purusha, the lower and upper nature of the supreme, procreates this maginificent world.

The present book, "the Dance of the Divinity, which is the third in the series of demystifying the Bhagavad Gita, focuses on the relationship between Nature and God. Lord says in chapter 13 that whatever exists in this world is because of the union of Prakriti and Purusha. What we perceive as reality is the projection of nature through sense organs in our mind interpreted through consciousness (called Maya in Vedanta) and understood as space-time reality by awareness.

Due to the magical spell of Maya, we believe that we are the doer of the acts performed by our bodies. Lord explains that this idea of agency to oneself is false, and the Prakriti (nature) acts due to its qualities with the power of the Supreme. The three attributes of the Prakriti, Satwik, Rajasik and Tamasik are responsible for the various kind of good and evil acts performed by the embodied.

One should seek the path treading which there is no return. That path leads to the Primaeval Man, the source of all this ancient universe extended everywhere. Here again, the Self, residing in the beings as their pure consciousness, is metaphorically described as the Primal Man or the Purusha.

Lord emphasises that while faith is a critical element for the evolution of a person, acting according to scriptures is also necessary. Knowledge of the scriptures keeps you on the right track and cautions you against erroneous practices like worshipping the dead and praying to ghosts and spirits. They also advise you against gruesome austerities harmful to your body and mind. Lord further commend that one must act for the sake of duty without desiring anything in return. Again elaborating the concept of Sanyasa and Tyaga, Lord Krishna says that the abandonment of desire in actions is Samyasa or renunciation. Surrendering the fruits of all deeds is called Tyaga or relinquishment.

We observe that this section of the Gita clarifies many common mistaken beliefs. The foremost among them is regarding knowledge of the scriptures. We tend to believe that if I am a spiritual person and have complete faith in God, then knowledge of the scriptures may not be necessary. However, bare faith without knowledge may direct you in the wrong direction. We observe that people engage in worship of tombs of dead people, which is against the scriptural path. Following the virtuous teachings of a saint may be more rewarding than worshipping his tomb.

Some people promote leaving the world in search of peace. However, one must not abandon the world but the desire for fruit in his work.

Lord advises that one should constantly be aware of the Supreme as his true Self and surrender oneself to Him. Lord promises that he will take care of the well-being of such a person. This gurantees that the person is free from all anxiety and focuses on his efforts with maximum efficiency. This also aligns all cosmic forces of nature for the triumph of such a person.

Om tat sat.

Annexure-I

Pronunciation Guide for Verses

Like the Harvard-Kyoto scheme, the ITRANS Romanization does not use any diacritical sign not found on the common English-language computer keyboard, and it is quite easy to read and pick up. ITRANS scheme has been used to transliterate Sanskrit verses. The pronunciation guide is given below.

Vowels

Devnagari	ITRANS	Comment
अ	a	as sound of "a" in ahead, metal {short "a" }
आ	A/aa	as sound of "a" in arm, cart, bar or as sound of "i" in ice, bite, fire {long "a"}
इ	i	as sound of "i" in it, pencil, credible {short "i" }
ई	I/ii	as sound of "i" in if, give, mirror {long "i" } or as sound of "ee" in feet or esteem
उ	u	as sound of "u" in put, push, pull
ऊ	U/uu	as sound of "o" in soon, spoon, fool {long "u" } or as sound of "u" in rule
ए	e	as sound of "e" in egg, bed, merry or as sound of "a" in age, aim, came

ऐ	ai	as sound of "a" in crane
ओ	o	as sound of "o" in go, low
औ	au	similar to the sound of "ow" in owl (if pronounced as single syllable)
अं	M/.n/.m	as sound of "um" in number, sound of "um" as in jump or umbrella
अः	H	sound of "h" with hard stop
ऋ	RRi/R^i	distinct sound similar to guttural sound of "r" as in riddle
ॠ	RRI/R^I	sound of "a" as in cat
अँ	.N	as in Umm!

Consonants:

Devanagari consonant letters include an implicit 'a' sound. It must be represented explicitly in ITRANS system

Devnagari	ITRANS	Comment
क	ka	Sound of "k" as in come, seek.
ख	kha	Sound of "kh" as in khaki
ग	ga	Sound of "g" as in girl
घ	gha	Sound of "gh" as in aghast.
ङ	~Na	Sound of n as in monkey, puncture

च	cha	Similar to the sound of "ch" as in chum.
छ	Cha	Similar to the "ch" in chuck, but with the release of breath, or aspiration.
ज	ja	J as in jump
झ	jha	Similar to the sound of 'dgeh' as in hedgehog
ञ	~na	Similar to the sound of "n" in ranch
ट	ta	Similar to the sound of "t" as in term.
ठ	tha	Similar to the sound of "th" as in foothold
ड	Da	Sound of "d" as in done
ढ	Dha	Sound of "dh"as in redhead
ण	Na	Sound of "n" using middle palate.
त	ta	Sound of "t"in Russian word glasnost
थ	tha	Sound of "th" in thanks
द	da	Sound of "th" as mother
ध	dha	Sound of "dh" as in dharma

न	na	Sound of "n" as in nut
प	pa	Sound of "p" as in pub
फ	pha	Sound similar to that of "f" in firm but with both lips touching each other.
ब	ba	Sound of "b" as in but
भ	bha	a sound of "b" using lips and saying "b" and "h" together as in "bhaji"
म	ma	Sound of "m" as in mother
य	ya	Sound of y as in yes
र	ra	Sound of "r" as in run
ल	la	Sound of "l" as in luck
व	va	Sound of "v" as in vulture
श	sha	Sound of "sh" as in shun
ष	Sha	close to the sound of "ssio" as in mission (sound of "sh" with back palate)
स	sa	Sound of "s" as in sun

ह	ha	Sound of "h" as in hub

Irregular Consonant Clusters

क्ष	kSha	Sound of "ctio" as in dictionary
त्र	tra	Sound of "tr" as in perestroika
ज्ञ	j~na	Sound of "gy" as in Magyar
श्र	shra	Sound of "shr" as in shred

www.ingramcontent.com/pod-product-compliance
Lightning Source LLC
LaVergne TN
LVHW091308150826
845673LV00006B/1575

* 9 7 8 9 3 5 6 8 0 6 6 7 2 *